HALFORDS

COMPLETE
MOTORING
▶▶▶ GUIDE ◀◀◀

Sue Baker

Published exclusively for Halford's Limited
Icknield Street Drive
Washford West
Redditch
Worcestershire
B98 0DE

by Martin Books
Simon & Schuster Consumer Group
Fitzwilliam House
32 Trumpington Street
Cambridge
CB2 1QY

ISBN 0 85941 748 4

First published 1991

Design and page make-up: Ken Vail Graphic Design
Illustrations: Richard Jacobs
Printed and bound by Rotolitho Lombarda s.p.a., Italy

Contents

Preface

Cars are fun but infuriating. They give us our freedom, but can let us down. They give us the richness of easy travel, but can keep us poor. They are faithful friends, but sometimes temperamental, occasionally traumatic.

How well your car serves you depends to a large extent on how you look after it, and how knowledgeably and intelligently you drive it. This book is intended to help you know it better, take as good care of it as possible, and make the best use of it.

I love cars, and have done for as long as I can remember. My enthusiasm for them grew from a childhood interest into an abiding passion and fruitful career. For this I must thank my father Frank Baker, whose enjoyment of cars brushed off so indelibly on his daughter. I am grateful, too, to David McCulloch, former motoring editor of the Kentish Times newspaper group, for his friendship and encouragement at the time when the road to a career as a motoring writer was far rockier for a woman than it is now. Most of all I thank my husband John Downing and children Ian and Hannah for their cheerful support during the writing of this book. I dedicate it to them and to everyone who enjoys cars.

Sue Baker
Chislehurst, 1991

Acknowledgements

The author wishes to thank the following people, companies and organisations for their assistance and encouragement in the preparation of this book: Halfords Limited; Camilla Simmons, senior commissioning editor, and Deborah Savage, managing editor, Martin Books; Stephen Adamson of Adamson Books; Ted Clements, chief examiner, Institute of Advanced Motorists; Erik Carlsson of Saab for his wisdom about winter driving; the Society of Motor Manufacturers and Traders; the Automobile Association; and my family, for their tolerance during the gestation.

The joy of driving

Have car, will travel. One of the great freedoms of modern life is being able to travel at will: to get into a car, turn the key, and go where the mood takes you. That is the joy of motoring. It is a freedom which many of us tend to take for granted, but we should never forget how liberating it is to be able to drive.

This is a book for those of us for whom driving still has an element of pleasure, excitement and discovery. People who simply regard a car as a means of getting from A to B, and who treat time on the road as a chore, miss so much of the enjoyment that motoring can bring.

I have never forgotten the thrill of my first few moments behind the wheel of a car, aged 15 and sternly tutored by my father as I steered the family saloon across the sand at low tide on a Welsh beach. Or the heady sense of achievement as I became the owner of my first car, an elderly Ford which was quickly to become notorious with my friends for its penchant for breaking down.

Cars may be inanimate machines, but our relationship with them, and dependence on them, is such that they seem to acquire personalities of their own. Why else do many owners give their cars nicknames, as exploited in one car maker's famous advertising slogan, 'What's yours called?'

We should see our cars as friends. If only everyone treated their cars with the care, respect and consideration they would show to their best friends, the roads would be much safer. A neglected car is an accident awaiting a location.

If the car you are driving is the first you have ever owned, try to remember how you feel about it now and carry that sense of responsibility right through your driving lifetime. If it is just the latest in a line of vehicles, make it your aim to treat it as well as the first one you ever bought.

For all this, a car is a machine, and cannot be expected to carry on performing faultlessly day after day unless it receives regular care, routine maintenance and periodic servicing. Lack of attention will turn it into a fickle and unreliable travelling companion, liable to let you down at the least convenient moment. So be prepared to spend a little time and money in keeping your car in perfect health. Cutting corners on maintenance is false economy and potentially hazardous.

Above all enjoy your car, and with the help of this book arm yourself with the knowledge to make the most of your motoring. With a sense of adventure and a car key in your hand, life need never be dull.

Preparation

There is a wry little jibe that trips readily off the tongue of anyone in the business of repairing machines when they are confronted with a careless owner; it goes: 'When in doubt, read the handbook'. Washing machine engineers mutter it when called to unclog a filter which the handbook advises should be checked weekly. Lawnmower repairers think it when putting right the damage caused by someone who has neglected to oil it as specified.

Most of us are pretty bad at reading handbooks, and no exception is made for those supplied with cars. So don't fall into a common trap. Make a point of reading everything the handbook has to say, and getting to know your car as thoroughly as possible.

Where cars are concerned, familiarity tends to breed not contempt, but complacency. We are so used to the convenience and reliability of modern cars that it is all too tempting to jump in and drive off as if nothing will ever go wrong. But sometimes it will, and it is sensible to prepare well for longer journeys, and to keep a trouble-shooter kit permanently in the car. Problems can arise even on short trips.

Always ensure that the jack and the complete toolkit supplied with the car are in it, so that, for example, a puncture need not turn into a major breakdown for lack of a wheel-brace to change the wheel. Also, keep a torch in the car to cope with any problems that arise at night.

A warning triangle is invaluable for your safety, as a warning to other drivers if the car is stopped at the roadside. Every car should carry a first-aid kit, not only to give immediate aid to anyone hurt in an accident, but also for tackling minor ailments such as insect stings.

A set of booster cables (jump leads) tucked in a corner of the boot can save a lot of time and trouble if you ever accidentally leave the car parked with the lights left on – and most of us make that mistake at some time or another.

Never travel without a good road atlas in the car, even on short journeys. A sudden diversion due to road closure caused by an incident ahead can be very time-consuming without a map to find the way back on course.

It may seem obvious to say it, but do keep a few coins and a phonecard permanently stowed (out of sight) in the car. It is all too easy to pop out on a short trip, not expecting to need any money, and then be stuck for change to call for help if the car lets you down.

Route planning

Always take time and trouble to plan your route thoroughly. Use a reliable map and familiarise yourself with the route to avoid needless diversions. Getting lost raises the stress level and puts you in even greater difficulty than you have already, if you are unlucky enough to break down and don't know where you are.

There is an enormous variety of scale, detail and presentation on offer in maps and atlases. The important thing is to choose one with which you feel completely comfortable. Many people who find navigating their way about the country difficult could help themselves by changing to a different map.

Map reading made easy

Here are a few basic rules to map-reading which can do a great deal to help make it easier:

➜ Make sure the map you use is a good, up-to-date one, so that any newly opened stretches of road, especially motorways, are included. Outdated maps are a recipe for getting lost, so replace your road atlas every so often.

➜ Always keep the map the same way up, and never be tempted to turn it this way and that to follow the road you are on. Although turning the map round may seem to help, it can quickly disorientate you, and is a classic reason why some people get lost trying to follow a map.

➜ If you have a long journey to do and need to use an unfamiliar map, spend a little time poring over it and getting familiar with its markings, symbols and scale. Above all, make sure you have taken in the scale: if you get across a map faster than you expect to, you're bound to get in a mess.

➜ When choosing a map, take time to find one which you can read easily, and put it to the test by looking at an area you know well, checking how easily you can pick out familiar routes on it. If a map is not easy to read in daylight, it is going to be much worse to follow on a wet night along a country lane in a moving car.

➜ When planning a long journey over unfamiliar country, make a list of town names and road numbers for the route you plan to use, and tape it onto the dashboard for easy reference while following road signs.

If you still find maps intimidating even after taking the advice given here, take heart. In cars of the future we will not need them. Satellite navigation is the coming thing, and one day we will simply follow instructions on a little TV monitor on the dashboard.

Safe driving

Driving may be fun but it is also a skill and a responsibility. If we all drove constantly with the care, attention and restraint we show whenever there is a police car in the vicinity, there would be far fewer accidents.

Passing the test is not the end of learning to drive, it is just the beginning. Experience should make us better drivers, but it also allows bad habits to creep in. Always maintain a critical and analytical attitude to your own driving, and ask someone close to you whose driving you respect to point out any flaws in your driving – and do the same for them.

Being at the wheel of a car should never be treated as a macho activity, nor as a casual one. In careless hands a car is potentially dangerous. Take a pride in being a safe driver.

Health and fitness

Are you fit to drive? Even a common cold can put you below par and take the edge off your concentration. I am not suggesting that a passing snuffle should automatically prevent someone from driving, but it should be treated as a signal to take extra care.

Everyone has 'off' days, when they wake up feeling tetchy and at odds with the world. But if you drive when you are feeling bad, you become an accident risk. Ask yourself whether you would want to be driven by someone else who felt the way you are feeling.

Some proprietary drugs, like antihistamines for hay fever and certain cold symptom suppressants, are notorious for their sleep-inducing side-effects. If you need something to treat a cold, or to counteract hayfever, make sure the brand you use is one of those which do not cause drowsiness. Whenever you are being prescribed drugs by a doctor, ask about any adverse effects on driving, and stick strictly to any guidelines given. Even common painkillers may have a marginal effect on your driving performance, so avoid taking them immediately before driving.

Be extra careful if you are in a state where you are liable to start sneezing at the wheel. An average sneeze lasts about five seconds, diverting the driver's attention for around 100 metres in a car travelling along a motorway at 70 mph. It is impossible to sneeze without closing your eyes, making you blind for some of that time – a chilling thought.

Even feeling just a bit cramped and achey on a long drive is a danger sign which should not be ignored. Cramp, or a dull ache in the back, shoulders or legs, is a clear warning that your circulation is sluggish, your concentration is slipping, and it is time for a break from the wheel. Stop as soon as possible, get out, breathe deeply and stretch your legs away from the car. Even a brief break can work wonders in refreshing you and restoring your level of concentration for the rest of the drive.

Exercises

Don't fume and fret in a traffic jam. Use the time spent sitting still in traffic by exercising to improve your level of concentration and general comfort when the traffic starts moving again. Do the same during a stop on a long journey.

Driver's exercises

→ Swing your head through big, lazy circles (1).

→ Exaggeratedly 'shrug' your shoulders.

→ Flex and circle your wrists in both directions.

→ Alternately tense and relax your leg muscles.

→ Stretch your toes and circle your ankles.

→ Clasp your hands together with the fingers interwoven, and first push the palms together (2), then try to pull them apart without releasing them (3).

If you notice other drivers giving you strange looks while you are going through your repertoire of exercises, just smile back. Flexing your muscles in a traffic jam is one great way of releasing tension and reducing the stress, and smiling at other drivers is another.

Drink

There is really only one thing to say about drinking and driving. Don't do it. Driving even slightly intoxicated endangers not just your licence, but your life and other people's. It simply is not worth the risk.

One of the commonest mistakes is the belief that it is safe to drink a little. Just a couple of drinks may not put you over the legal limit, but it will almost certainly dull your reactions just enough to make the difference between responding instantly to an emergency situation, or becoming a victim of what should have been an avoidable accident.

Alcohol has a long-lasting effect. Drivers have been caught out by taking a taxi to and from a party, and then being caught still over the limit while driving themselves to work the next morning. If in any doubt, don't drive.

Low-alcohol wines and beers are a very useful alternative for drivers, but it can still important to be careful about the quantity consumed. Although they contain less alcohol than normal wines or beers, they still have enough to create a cumulative effect and put you over the drink-drive limit if you consume enough.

Attitude

Airline pilots are warned to beware of starting a flight in a bad mood, such as being preoccupied by a domestic argument before leaving home. Drivers should heed the same advice. Far more accidents happen through driver error than ever occur due to mechanical failures, and an angry or irritable driver is a potentially dangerous one.

Everyone who drives should try to avoid confrontations with traffic wardens, or fist-shaking at some stupid oaf who has just cut you up at a roundabout, or nipped into a parking space ahead of you. In such situations take a deep breath, and swallow your irritation – and your pride. Responding irritably or aggressively simply isn't worth the risk.

Fatigue

Tiredness is insidious, it creeps up on you. Because we all assume that accidents are things which only happen to other people, we may tend to overlook the early symptoms of weariness. But it is vital to recognise them: the few moments here and there when your mind starts to wander, your reactions begin to feel dulled and a slightly detached feeling develops.

By then you have probably already ignored the common sense advice of motoring organisations, who regularly caution us not to drive more than a couple of hours at a stretch, and at the most three. A break from the wheel for a cup of coffee, or simply a stroll around in the fresh air, can work wonders.

Even if you start a drive fully fresh and alert after a good night's sleep, the very act of driving for hours on end, sitting in the same position, and especially on the dreary sameness of a motorway, adds up to a perfect recipe for gnawing fatigue.

The dangers of being tired at the wheel are all too obvious, but how do you recognise when you're in the danger zone? If you feel fine when you climb into the car, how do you spot the warning signs? If you're driving a route you know well, you may find your brain engaging its automatic pilot, and following a course from habit. Ever realised you can't remember any of the last mile you've just driven? That's a danger sign to heed.

Translate the same set of circumstances on to a route you don't know, and the risks are multiplied. On a strange journey, a tired driver is at risk of simply not seeing a bend coming up, or not seeing a stationary object in time.

So here's my advice to avoid ever finding yourself in that situation:

➔ If you know you're really tired, don't drive. Delay the journey and get some rest first.

➔ When planning a long trip, time it so that you will start fresh rather than setting off to tackle a 200 miles trip straight after work. Better to get an early night and set off really early in the morning, before much traffic is about.

➔ If you must go somewhere at the end of a hard day, then try to allow yourself at least half an hour's unwinding time for a cup of coffee or tea and a light snack before setting off.

➔ Alternatively, shoot smartly away from work to avoid the traffic (sitting in jams is stressful and fatiguing) and then stop for a breather and coffee after only an hour at the wheel.

➔ Avoid heavy meals just before or during a journey. Your body diverts blood to a full stomach in order to work on digestion, leaving less for the brain, which then feels drowsy.

➔ On the other hand, never start a day's driving without something inside you. Drivers should never skip, or even skimp, on breakfast. Regular light snacks while on a long journey help ensure that the body's blood-sugar level doesn't dip too low, which can have a bad affect on concentration.

➔ Keep the car cool and well ventilated. Better to wrap up warmly and have the heating low, than to wear thin clothes and then need the heater on full blast. A car full of hot air makes you sluggish, dries your eyes and increases fatigue.

➔ Wear several thin but warm layers rather than a bulky overcoat. Being comfortable and relaxed is an important fatigue-avoidance aid.

➔ Counteract the effects of fatigue on a long, boring drive, such as when travelling distances on a motorway, by choosing a stimulating radio programme to listen to, by deliberately checking the instruments at regular intervals, by talking to other passengers and by setting yourself mental exercises to help keep you alert.

➔ Avoid gazing endlessly forward at the ribbon of road stretching ahead. Deliberately switch your gaze from the car just in front of you to distant objects, to road signs, and so on, to exercise your eyes.

➔ If you know you're tired but there's no choice, you have to drive, then keep the driving seat upright, have a window open, keep the air in the car on the chilly side and play rousing music on the stereo.

Good driving

The key to successful, safe driving is a keen awareness of everything going on around you, and the ability to filter out less urgent inputs so as to be able to react to those which should be given priority. For example, when approaching a hazard with a talkative passenger in the seat beside you, it is vital to be able to shut out the chat and give your full attention to what is happening on the road.

Three words sum up what is required of a good driver: observation, concentration, anticipation.

Be constantly on the look-out for unexpected actions from other road-users and pedestrians. How many potential hazards can you spot?

Observation is vital: this means not just seeing what is happening as far ahead as the back bumper of the car in front, but looking way down the road for clues to anything which may affect your safe progress, as well as being aware of what is going on around and behind the car.

Allowing your attention to stray while at the wheel is potentially dangerous. Driving demands total concentration, and nothing should be allowed to compromise it.

A good driver anticipates well ahead. For example, he or she will look for feet under a parked lorry which may warn of someone about to step out into the road, or will gauge the direction of the road beyond a bend from a line of trees or telegraph poles.

You and the law

There are a number of ways in which a driver may run foul of the law. Here is a basic checklist for staying out of trouble:

➔ Keep the car scrupulously maintained. Worn tyres, tired shock absorbers, faulty lights and a badly corroded underbody are just some of the illegal items which may risk an unwelcome brush with the police.

➔ Make sure all your documents are kept up to date and available for inspection. You must have a valid licence, insurance, tax disc and, if the car is over three years old, an MOT certificate.

➔ Watch your speed and obey the limit. Being caught speeding risks an expensive fine and points on your licence.

➔ Be careful where you park. Leaving your car on the zig-zag lines approaching a pedestrian crossing is illegal because it puts others at risk.

➔ Switch on to dipped headlamps on unlit roads at night and in poor visibility during the day.

Car documents

This collection of paperwork must be kept up to date:

➔ Driving licence – it must be valid for the type of vehicle you are driving, and should be carried with you.

➔ Insurance – carry the certificate or cover note relevant to the car.

➔ Road tax – a valid tax disc should be displayed in the bottom nearside corner of the windscreen. It is illegal to be with out one, and contrary to popular misconception you do not have 14 days' grace to renew it.

➔ MOT – an MOT (Ministry of Transport) test certificate is a legal requirement for every car more than three years old.

➔ Registration document – evidence of a car's ownership. Keep it safe at home, *not* in the car.

Your should also have a service book that was supplied with the car to show the intervals at which it is serviced. Ask to have it stamped each time your car goes in to the garage for attention: it will be a valuable asset as proof of mileage and good maintenance when you sell the car. Likewise, garage bills for the cost of maintaining and repairing the car are a useful record to show to a prospective buyer.

Insurance

If we were all perfect drivers, living in a world with no crime and no risk of fire, there would be no need for car insurance. However, life isn't like that, and we do need the protection of a good insurance policy to look after us and our cars. But there is no reason to pay more than absolutely necessary. Motor insurance rates can vary enormously, so it is worth shopping around to find the best price available.

There are of course several ways in which you could easily slice your premium at a stroke – changing your treasured Ferrari for a modest little Fiesta, for example, or uprooting from Fulham and moving to Falmouth. Unfortunately, such major modifications in the risk you can present to a prospective insurer are rarely practical. Neither can you do much about your age, which is also a factor in the insurance company's equation when working out the premium. But there are some aspects of risk which you can control, such as renting a lock-up garage if the car would otherwise be parked overnight in the street (though the rental costs may exceed the saving in premium), or restricting the number of drivers, preferably to just yourself and one other.

Opting for third party, fire and theft instead of fully comprehensive cover can also bring down the cost, but is invariably false economy. If the cost of comprehensive cover is hard to stomach, how much more so will be the cost of repairing a badly damaged car with no help from an insurance policy?

Shopping around for the best policy can be tedious, time-consuming and frustrating, but you can get a good, reliable insurance broker to do it for you. If he is good at his job, he will have the experience to carve a path through the bewildering array of policies on offer, and find the one best tailored to your needs.

Do make sure, though, that the broker is reputable. The British Insurance Brokers Association, Bibi House, 10 Bevis Marks, London EC3 (071-623 9043) will help in finding a member broker near to you.

There are other ways to find the best insurance deal:

➜ Investigate any special insurance schemes which may be available through your work.

➜ Check through a franchised dealer whether there is a special scheme relevant to your make of car.

➜ Take an advanced driving test. The Institute of Advanced Motorists has negotiated discounted insurance rates for its members.

Some insurance companies regard women as a better risk than men, or have special rates for older drivers. If relevant, find a company that offers these discounts.

Before deciding on any policy, check what it includes. No-claims bonus protection and cover for a broken windscreen are worth having, but are by no means automatic.

Finally, remember that the validity of an insurance policy also depends on a car being maintained in a good, roadworthy condition. A badly worn tyre, out-of-date MOT or worn-out brake pads could invalidate your cover.

Buying and selling a car

Buying a car should be enjoyable, but it can be a minefield for the unwary. Be prepared to invest time and research into getting the best deal, whether you are buying or selling.

Choosing a new car

There are various simple rules to bear in mind before you write out that large cheque.

DO ✔

✔ Gather as much information as possible on the cars you are considering. Compare warranties and any special offers.

✔ Spend time visiting showrooms to compare features.

✔ Insist on a test-drive before making your choice.

✔ Try more than one dealer to find the best deal, especially if you are trading in your old car.

✔ Compare building society and bank rates before deciding on a credit deal offered by the garage.

DON'T ✗

✗ Be afraid to ask for a discount. The dealer may well have scope to negotiate on the price, but is unlikely to offer to do so unless you ask.

✗ Be rushed into making a decision. For most of us buying a car is the most expensive purchase we will make after buying a house, so take time to think.

When buying second-hand

DO ✔

✔ Go car-hunting in daylight. In the dark it is much harder to spot potentially costly flaws.

✔ Carry a magnet. A car that looks superficially wonderful may in fact be held together with masses of filler. Any bits of the bodywork which don't attract the magnet are not metal but glass fibre filler.

✔ Carry a mirror to inspect parts of the under-body you cannot easily see, and look for signs of corrosion.

✔ Take with you a good critical friend with some mechanical knowledge, who may spot faults you don't, and who will be sufficiently detached from the excitement of the prospective purchase to talk you out of buying a rogue car you have fallen in love with.

✔ Check the dip-stick. If the oil is black and sooty-looking, it has not been changed recently enough, which suggests that the car's maintenance may have been skimped.

✔ Ask to see service records, such as garage bills, as evidence of the car's regular maintenance and proof of mileage.

✓ Open and shut the doors a few times, to look for signs of mis-alignment which could be the clue to a crash repair. Look for other symptoms too, like minute specks of paint where they shouldn't be, such as on the windscreen rubber, telling the story of a respray.

✓ Look for blue smoke puffing out of the exhaust when you start up, which suggests engine wear that could be very expensive to remedy.

✓ Check for worn tyres, including the spare. Your safety depends on them being in tip-top condition, and replacements are costly.

✓ Insist on a test drive. With the engine running and the handbrake on, engage third gear and lift the clutch pedal slowly. The engine should stall straight away. If it doesn't, it tells you that the clutch is slipping.

✓ Try selecting top gear at around 25 miles an hour, and then put your foot hard down on the accelerator. If the engine complains loudly with a heavy knocking noise, it's a sign of worn big-end bearings. The bill for replacing them could hurt.

DON'T ✗

✗ Assume that a recent MOT certificate guarantees the car is in good condition and worth buying. It is only evidence of very basic road-worthiness on a particular day.

✗ Be impressed by mats or extra carpeting put in on top of the car's original carpets, and seat covers not part of the original equipment. Either may hide tell-tale signs of a weary car.

✗ Assume that a wonderfully shiny looking engine denotes a prime condition car. It could just mean that the engine bay has been steam-cleaned.

✗ Buy in wet weather, when rain makes the bodywork look glossier and discourages you from examining the car as carefully as you otherwise might.

✗ Trust any seller who helpfully suggests bringing the car to you when you have rung up in response to an advertisement . Ask for the address and say you'll come and see it, so that you know where the person selling the car lives, if you do decide to buy it and have trouble later.

When selling your old car

DO ✓

✓ Give it a top-to-toe valeting. First appearances count.

DON'T ✗

✗ Leave any prospective buyer alone with the car and keys.

✗ Hand over the car or registration document until you have the full agreed price in cash or the cheque has been cleared.

✗ Forget to detach and send off the registration change of ownership to the DVLA at Swansea.

✗ Leave any personal possessions in the car when you hand it over.

Know your car

It is possible to be a good driver without ever knowing what goes on under the bonnet, but it is much more difficult. Getting the best from your car, and taking the best possible care of it as an owner, does require at least the rudiments of mechanical knowledge.

Modern cars are highly sophisticated and complex machines, constructed of around 4,000 or more component parts. The mere sight of the engine compartment is enough to deter many motorists, who regard a car's innards as a perplexing mystery and would rather leave any involvement with them to the nearest garage. Enthusiasts used to take real pleasure from working on their cars, but today only a determinedly knowledgeable do-it-yourself whizz embarks on his or her own car servicing. Most of us now do little more than routine maintenance, and let the garage do the rest.

Learning about the basics of how a car works may be daunting for the unmechanically minded, but it can make you a better driver and enables you to look after your car more efficiently. It also helps in spotting the early clues when something is going wrong, when swift action can save a bigger bill later. Even if you have not the least intention of dirtying your hands under the bonnet, appreciating what happens there is very satisfying and helps cultivate a mechanical sympathy which will enable you to treat your car better and help it last longer. It also makes you better equipped to deal with the garage when the car goes in for servicing or repairs.

So even if things mechanical are a bit of an anathema to you, as they are to many people, don't skip over this chapter. A little knowledge is by no means a dangerous thing.

The engine

The engine is the heart of the car, its driving force. Its basic function is to convert fuel into the mechanical energy which will create and sustain motion. In other words, it provides the power which enables the car to move.

The method by which it does this has been in use for over a century, and is known as 'internal combustion'. Fuel is burned inside the engine cylinders to create pressure which produces mechanical movement.

In the majority of cars the engine is at the front, and fuel is fed to it from a tank normally located at the back – kept as far distant from the engine as possible to minimise fire risk.

Fuel is pumped from the tank to the carburettor or injection system, where it is mixed with air to form an explosive mixture. This mixture is

Parts of the engine

Carburettor: device which vaporises petrol and mixes it with air.
Injection system: alternative to carburettor, squirts measured quantities of petrol into engine.
Cylinder: container in which piston moves up and down.
Piston: component which slides inside cylinder to transfer combustion energy.
Valve: device which controls entry of petrol-air mixture or exit of exhaust gases.
Crankshaft: metal shaft which transmits drive power.
Sump: oil container at base of engine.
Turbocharger: device driven by exhaust gases to speed flow of petrol-air mixture into engine.

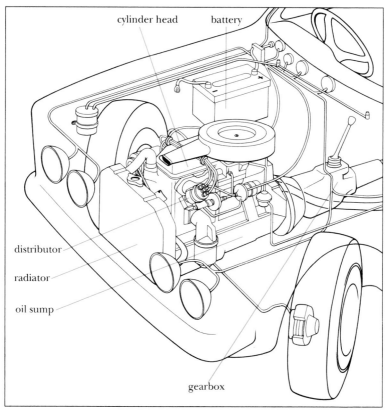

cylinder head   battery

distributor

radiator

oil sump

gearbox

compressed by the pistons inside the engine cylinders, and then ignited by a spark of electric current supplied from the spark plugs.

As the mixture explodes it turns to gases which force the pistons down, which in turn rotate a shaft to which they are attached. This is the crankshaft, specially designed to transmit the power created in the engine to where it will be used to propel the car. It passes the power through the gearbox to the drive shaft and ultimately to the wheels to turn them.

1 Induction stroke   2 Compression stroke

3 Power stroke   4 Exhaust stroke

The way an engine works: 1, Air/fuel mixture enters the cylinder through an inlet valve. 2, The piston compresses it. 3, A spark ignites it. 4, Ignition forces the piston down and waste gases exit through the exhaust valve.

Engine designs vary considerably, but the basic structure consists of a metal cylinder block which houses the pistons, and a cylinder head bolted on top. Attached below the cylinder block is the sump, which collects the oil circulated through the engine to lubricate the moving parts.

At the top of the engine block, situated above the cylinders, is a system of valves which open and close to allow the fuel-air mixture to enter the combustion chambers, and exhaust gases to be expelled from them.

A typical car engine has four cylinders, but the more cylinders, the more powerful the car, twelve being the maximum. Another feature that affects a car's performance is the number of valves on each cylinder. Traditionally there would be just two, one inlet and one exhaust, but many cars now have 'multi-valve' engines, typically with two inlet and two exhaust valves. This increases the efficiency of the combustion process and thus raises the output of power.

Waste gases from the combustion process are removed from the engine through the exhaust system, and expelled into the atmosphere via the tailpipe at the back of the car. Some modern cars have a turbocharger attached to the exhaust system. In this, the gases leaving the engine are used to drive a turbine, which then pressurises the fuel-air mixture entering the engine and so increases the power it produces.

You control the power produced from your engine with your foot. The harder you push down on the accelerator pedal, the faster the flow of fuel to the engine, and hence the greater the output of power, and the more energy to turn the wheels.

In the majority of cars the power is supplied to only one pair of wheels, either the front pair as in front-wheel-drive, or to the rear pair in a rear-wheel-drive car. A smaller number of cars have four-wheel-drive, commonly known as 4x4, in which all the wheels are powered by the engine.

The gearbox

Power created inside the engine and passed along the crankshaft has to be transmitted to the wheels, to enable them to turn and move along the road. To do so, it passes either through a gearbox or through the automatic transmission, both of which control the power coming from the engine and manage the rate at which it is allowed, via the drive shaft, to turn the wheels.

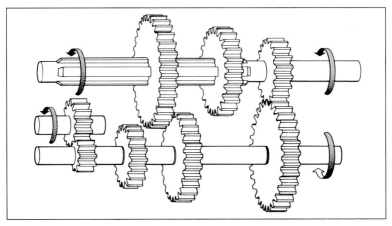

How gears work. Toothed cogs on the input shaft (top, connected to the engine) mesh with other cogs on the gear shaft (below, connected to the back axle). The larger the cog on the input shaft and the smaller the cog it meshes with, the faster the car will travel for a given engine speed.

The gearbox is essential to harness the engine power and allow it to be used to cope with changing driving conditions such as varying terrain, including hills. Imagine trying to climb a hill in a car with no gears. The engine could be racing and turning out considerable power, but lack the force to push the car up the hill, rather like a person sweating hard to push a boulder that is too big for them to move. The gears enable the engine force to be harnessed either as power, needed to start the car or get it uphill, or as speed. In the former the wheels move comparatively slowly in relation to the speed of the engine, thereby enabling the car to overcome the inertia of its own weight and haul itself up the hill.

But if the car were set to do this permanently, without gears, then fast engine speed could not subsequently be turned into fast wheel speed, and your car would always be very slow.

Parts of the gearbox

Gear: toothed disc which meshes with another to transmit power or movement from one shaft to another.
Clutch: mechanical device which connects and disconnects the drive from the engine to the road wheels.
Torque converter: a type of automatic clutch.

With a manual gearbox, the driver is in control of the power supplied to the wheels and uses the gearstick to decide what happens inside the gearbox.

By selecting a low gear, you are choosing to slow down the speed at which the wheels are turning, in relation to the engine speed. This enables the car to exert the force needed to pull away from stationary, or to overcome gravity in driving up a hill.

When you select a higher gear, the speed of the wheels is more closely related to that of the engine. This enables the car to be run at a lower rate of combustion, or reduced engine revolutions ('revs') when it has already built up its momentum.

In a car with automatic transmission, the gearbox changes gear without any direct control from the driver. There is a device called a torque converter attached to the crankshaft, which works through centrifugal force to engage the drive when the engine reaches a certain speed. A special fluid is pumped through a series of valves which trigger the gears to change in response to the engine speed.

An automatic car has only two pedals, the accelerator and brake. There is no need for a clutch pedal, because a clutch is only needed for the process of changing gear manually.

Clutch

The clutch acts as a bridge between the engine and the gearbox in a car with manual transmission. It is a necessary interface between the engine, which runs constantly all the time the car is in use, and the transmission, which sometimes has to be stationary, as when the car stops in traffic.

The main component of the clutch is a spring-loaded disc which is faced with a special friction material, and which pushes tightly against a metal flywheel attached to the end of the crankshaft. For most of the time the clutch disc rotates freely with the flywheel, and allows the components inside the gearbox to rotate as well. But when you push down on the clutch pedal, you cause a lever to disconnect the clutch plate from the flywheel, which in turn stops movement inside the gearbox. This allows a different gear to be selected through the gearstick, which is then engaged when you release, or 'let out', the clutch pedal again.

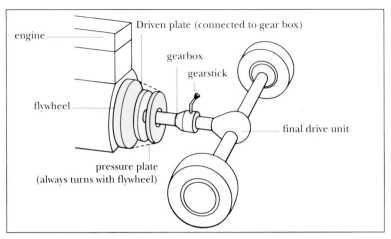

The clutch mechanism consists of steel plates and a flywheel. When the clutch pedal is pushed down, it releases pressure on the plates (as above) and disengages the gearbox from the engine, to allow the gear to be changed.

When the clutch pedal is depressed (or if the gearbox is in neutral with none of the gears engaged), the engine's power, as transmitted to the flywheel, is disconnected from the wheels. That is why the clutch pedal should never be kept fully or partially depressed while the car is in motion – a bad habit known as 'riding' the clutch, because it means that power from the engine is temporarily severed from the wheels and is not being used to control the car.

Steering

The direction the car takes is controlled by its steering. As you turn the steering wheel, your action is transmitted along the shaft to which the wheel is attached. At the base of the shaft is a gear mechanism with a rack and pinion connecting it to another shaft,

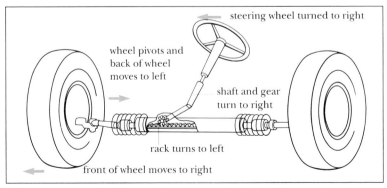

In rack and pinion steering, the most common type, the circular movement of the steering wheel is turned into lateral movement along the axle, which then changes the forward angle of the wheels.

and this enables your movement in turning the steering wheel to be translated into sideways movement on the horizontal shaft.

Rods are attached to each end of that horizontal shaft, and as it moves to left or right they push or pull against the mechanisms holding the front wheels, to turn the wheels in the direction in which you are turning the wheel.

Most cars are steered by the front wheels only, but a few cars now have a system of four-wheel-steering. This is designed to make parking easier by enabling the car to turn more tightly, which is useful in negotiating a small gap, and to improve stability when taking a corner at speed, as it points all the wheels in the same direction.

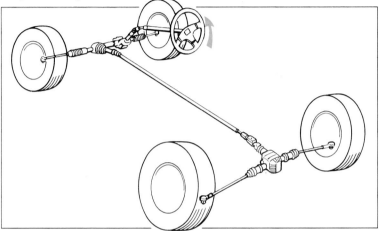

In four-wheel steering, the back wheels are steered as well as those at the front. Normally, as shown, they all turn in the same direction. At low speeds, as when parking, they turn in opposite directions.

Suspension

A car without suspension would be very uncomfortable, with every bump and dip in the road surface transmitted directly through the car's structure to bounce you brutally as you drove along.

Not only this, but it would also be dangerous. If the car were so rigidly fixed to its wheels that it pitched and tossed with every surface bump, there would be the risk that all its wheels would lose contact with the road from time to time, and it would be very difficult to keep under control.

The suspension is therefore designed to absorb the pitching and bumps from potholes and undulations over which the car travels. It works basically by means of a spring at each corner of the car, placed between the hub assembly holding the wheel, and the section of car body above it.

This spring assembly is known as a shock absorber, quite simply because it absorbs shocks which would otherwise be transmitted from the road to the car body, and ultimately to you inside the car.

The spring is 'dampened' so that it quickly goes back to stable after absorbing a bump, instead of continually bouncing.

That, in very simple terms, is how suspension works, but it is in reality rather more sophisticated than that. The system in a modern car has a number of other components designed to vary the angle of the wheel in relation to the road so as to provide the best absorption of shocks under different driving conditions, such as when the car dips forward under braking or leans under cornering.

The suspension itself only furnishes part of the shock-absorbing properties of a car. The tyres, inflated with air, do a certain amount to 'cushion' irregularities in the road surface, and springing and foam cushioning of the car seats also help soak up bumps before they reach the driver and passengers, as anyone who has sat in a car with ancient and worn seats will know.

Brakes

The engine powers the car's forward motion, and reducing engine power has the effect of slowing the car, which is known as 'engine braking'.

To reduce speed more effectively, the car also has a braking system designed to exert friction on the wheels and quickly cut down the rate at which they are turning.

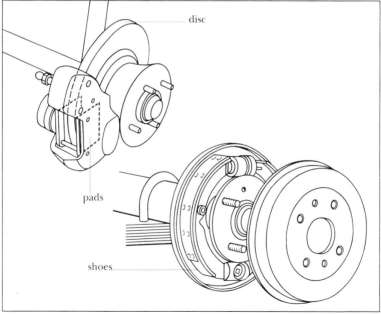

These are the two main types of brakes. A disc brake (top) works by means of a pair of pads which grip either side of a steel disc that forms part of the wheel. In a drum brake (below) a pair of brake shoes pushes outwards against the wheel drum.

This system is operated by means of hydraulics, with fluid transmitting pressure from the brake pedal, which is controlled by the driver, to the pads, which then exert stopping force on the wheels. The basic principle is not much different from that of bicycle brakes.

When you push down on the brake pedal, it has the effect of moving a piston inside a master cylinder and pushing hydraulic fluid through narrow pipes carried beneath the car to little cylinders at each wheel. As the fluid enters those cylinders, it makes the pistons inside them press against the brake pads. The pads are faced with a friction lining, and it is the contact between this lining and the brake drum or disc attached to the wheel that makes the wheel slow down. Drum brakes work in the same way, except that pads are replaced by brake shoes, which are pushed outwards to create braking force.

Some braking systems are made more effective by the use of 'servo assistance', which uses a difference in pressure between two chambers inside the 'servo' unit to help increase the braking effort. Because the vacuum that creates the difference in pressure is produced by the engine's power, this system is often called power-assisted braking.

The electrics

At the heart of a car's electrical system is the battery, which produces and stores the electricity needed to run the car. It creates electricity by a chemical reaction between internal lead plates and the sulphuric acid solution in which they are immersed, which is why you may sometimes hear it described as a lead-acid battery.

The chemical reaction causes lead to be released from one set of plates and deposited on another. To prevent one set of plates from becoming worn out, a supply of current is sent back to the battery all the time the car engine is running. A small generator driven by the engine, which is either a dynamo in older cars or an alternator in modern ones, feeds electricity back into the battery to reverse the lead-discharging process so that the chemical reaction can happen repeatedly.

Electrical current flows out from the battery through the 'live' or positive terminal, identified by a + sign, and through an insulated cable to the component of the car that needs power. The circuit is completed by current flowing back to the battery through a cable leading to the negative terminal, identified by a – sign, but on the way 'earthed' by a connector to the car's body.

A complex system of electrical wiring, known as the car's wiring loom, carries current around the car to power its various systems, such as the lights, wipers, heater fan, radio and so on.

As in the electrical wiring system in a house, the electrics in a car pass through a safety net of fuses, so that if a circuit is overloaded by a fault, it is the fuse which will burn out rather than the wiring.

The cooling system

By the very nature of the way in which it works, an engine heats up to a very high temperature. The combustion process, and friction occuring between the moving mechanical parts, generates a great deal of heat.

To stop the level of heat from becoming excessive, to reduce and control it, and to disperse it, there has to be an efficient cooling system. In a conventional car engine water is the prime means.

Water is circulated by being pumped through narrow passages inside the engine, passing all the areas where the most heat is generated, to absorb some of that heat and carry it away. The heated water then travels from the engine via rubber hoses to the radiator. There it disperses its heat by passing through the radiator's very large surface area; the radiator is positioned at the front of the car so that it can be cooled by the stream of cool air that constantly passes as the car moves. This cooling process is helped by a fan mounted behind the radiator.

As water under pressure can take a higher temperature than normal before boiling, the cooling system is pressurised, which is why the water gushes out like a mini-geyser when the system springs a leak. A thermostat controls the temperature at which the system operates, regulating the flow of water according to the way in which the car is being driven and the ambient temperature, depending on the time of year.

Antifreeze is added to the cooling system to prevent the water from freezing in winter and cracking the engine block; some antifreeze also has anti-corrosion properties. A useful by-product of the engine cooling system is warmth for the car interior. Air sucked in from outside the car is passed across a heat exchanger, like a tiny radiator behind the dashboard, which receives its heat from some of the engine coolant passing through. It is then transmitted into the car's passenger area.

Caring for your car

Cars are not cheap. For most of us, buying a car represents a major financial outlay, especially if it is new. It is also a feature in our lives which we tend to rely on, and we find it very inconvenient, even infuriating, when it lets us down. So there are very good reasons for taking good care of your car. Scrupulous maintenance and regular servicing will not actually guarantee that it will never break down, but they will go a long way towards encouraging reliability.

The other prime reason for good car care is a financial one. A well-maintained car, in good condition and with evidence of regular mechanical care in the form of a properly documented full service history, will sell more easily and command a better price than a neglected car.

Routine maintenance

Good maintenance on a regular basis is one of the vital keys to trouble-free car ownership. If your car seems to be behaving itself and never showing any signs of trouble, it is tempting to skimp on the regular routine checks. Most of us suffer from lack of time, forgetfulness or simple lethargy at one time or another, but letting these seduce us into neglecting routine car care is a potentially hazardous or costly mistake. It could, for example, result in your peering through a grubby windscreen on the motorway in filthy weather with no fluid left in the windscreen washer bottle. It could put your engine at risk of serious or even terminal damage because the oil level has dropped too low.

Observing the following checklist of tasks which need to be kept up to date, on a daily, weekly and monthly basis, will not take a lot of time but will save you trouble later.

Daily

➔ Clean the windscreen and any other windows which need attention, inside as well as out.

➔ Wipe the lights clean if they have been soiled, and check for any blown bulbs or cracked glass.

➔ Keep an eye on the petrol gauge, to check that the level of fuel in the tank does not drop too low. Running out of petrol is one of the most common breakdowns.

➡ Remove any rubbish inside the car. An unkempt car encourages sloppy driving habits.

➡ Keep an eye out for any oil leaks from the engine. If you see any they should always receive urgent attention.

Weekly

➡ Check the oil level. Do it with the engine cold, before driving anywhere, and while the car is parked on level ground. Remove the dipstick, wipe it clean, replace it into its slot, then remove it to check how far up the oil shows, which should be about halfway between the maximum and minimum marks. Top up as necessary.

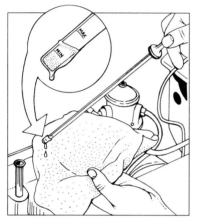
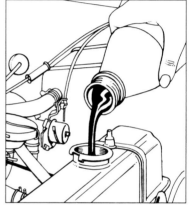

➡ Examine the tyres for signs of cuts or damage to the sidewalls. Check the pressures, including the spare, and add air as necessary.

➡ Unless the battery is one of the newer, maintenance-free kind, check the cells to ensure that the level of fluid covering them is at least a quarter of an inch above the metal plate. If any cells have a lower level, top them up with distilled or de-ionised water (never tap water).

➡ If you have any doubt about the battery's reliability, boost it with a trickle charge (a slow overnight charge) and consider replacing it.

➡ If your car does not have a sealed cooling system, undo the pressurised radiator cap while cold and top up as necessary with water. In the winter mix in the appropriate proportion of anti-freeze.

➡ Wash the car thoroughly, or treat it to a trip through a car-wash. Clean out the interior, shake out any floor mats and vacuum the carpets.

➡ Check for any signs of water leaks into the car, and especially in the boot, where water draining down into the spare wheel well can quickly encourage rust if left unattended.

➡ Top up the windscreen washer fluid.

Monthly

➜ Check the tyres for tread depth and any signs of uneven wear. They could mean that the wheels are out of alignment and need garage attention.

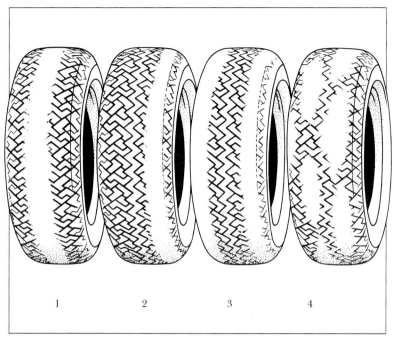

Diagnosing tyre wear. 1, Bald central strip, over-inflation. 2, One edge bald, wheel mis-aligned. 3, Both edges bald, under-inflation. 4, Uneven wear, suspension or brake defect.

➜ Test the shock absorbers by pressing down firmly on each corner of the car in turn. You should see it spring back up to where it started. If it feels soggy or see-saws more than once, the suspension needs attention.

➜ Examine the bodywork closely for any signs of rust spots forming, or stone-chips on the paintwork. Attend to them promptly with rust remover and touch up paint before they deteriorate further.

➜ Clean any dirt and grease off the battery terminals, and smear them with petroleum jelly to protect them from dirt and damp.

➜ Check all the water hoses under the bonnet for any signs of cracking or perishing, and ensure that all the hose clips are tight.

➜ Lubricate locks and hinges as recommended in the car handbook.

➜ Get down to check under the car for signs of corrosion and to ensure the exhaust pipe is sound, with no holes in the metal, and that it is securely fixed, with none of its mountings adrift.

➜ Clean out the boot and remove any non-essential items.

Servicing

Even though you are regularly checking all the things you should, your car still need periodic specialist attention to keep it running efficiently. Always stick to the servicing intervals recommended by the manufacturer.

Service schedule

What is included in a 'major' service depends on the specification from the individual manufacturer, but a typical service schedule would include most or all of these (topping up and lubrication carried out where necessary):

➔ Check bonnet safety catch.

➔ Check all lights and replace faulty bulbs.

➔ Check tyres, including spare, for condition and pressure.

➔ Check wheelnuts for tightness.

➔ Check battery terminals for tightness, and clean them.

➔ Check and top up engine coolant.

➔ Check and top up hydraulic fluid levels.

➔ Change wiper blades.

➔ Check and adjust screen washer jets.

➔ Change spark plugs.

➔ Change contact breaker points.

➔ Check and adjust valve clearances.

➔ Check and adjust ignition timing.

➔ Check condition of high-tension leads.

➔ Check and lubricate distributor.

➔ Check hoses for leaks and deterioration.

➔ Check and adjust throttle linkage.

➔ Change engine oil and filter.

➔ Change air filter.

➔ Check and top up rear axle oil.

➔ Check and adjust clutch pedal.

➔ Check and adjust handbrake.

➔ Check brake pads and linings for wear.

➔ Check brake pipes for leaks and wear.

➔ Check steering and suspension linkages for wear.

➔ Check exhaust system for leaks and wear.

The precise details of how often these service intervals are, and what each service includes, vary from one car to the next. Traditionally, a car used to have a routine lubrication service every six months, and a more extensive service including the brakes, steering and other major components every year, with oil changes at three monthly intervals. For most cars, that is no longer the case. Major service intervals once a year, or every 12,000 miles, have now become common for the majority of new cars, with a minor service and oil change sometimes specified in between.

Dealing with the garages

Do you grit your teeth with dread when it is time to book your car in for a service? At least you are in good company. Taking the car to the garage seems to rate on a par with an appointment at the dentist or an encounter with a tax inspector for many people.

The most common worries are about being presented with a bill far higher than bargained for, or being blinded by technicalities into agreeing to something not quite understood. Whether these happen may well depend on what you do when you take the car into the garage.

One way to avoid an unpleasant surprise about the cost is to be careful to ask in advance what the price will be, check whether or not that includes VAT, and insist that no additional work is carried out unless the garage seeks your prior permission by telephone. This way, you should at least have a clear idea of the expense to which you are committing yourself. Ask in advance what the labour charge per hour will be. It can vary greatly by car make and by garage location, so if you feel it is too high, try somewhere else.

Find out whether the garage adds any little extras, such as a set charge for 'consumables' – by which they mean a mopping-up charge for small items such as washers and bolts, or the plastic cover used to protect your seat from the mechanic's dirty overalls.

Ask for a list of all the items included on the service schedule, so that at least you know what is supposed to be done.

Some garages now offer servicing on a 'menu pricing' system, meaning that there is a set price for a set list of servicing items. It is a good idea as the customer will know in advance precisely what work will be carried out, and the pre-agreed cost, so it is worth trying to find a garage that operates the system.

Always be careful about leaving too much to the discretion of the garage. If you complain, for example, of spongy brakes and ask them to sort out the problem without discussing cost, then the resulting bill may make you wince. Ask instead that they advise you of what they think is wrong, and how much it will cost to put right, before the work goes ahead.

It may not save you any money, because the problem, especially if it involves something as crucial to your safety as the brakes, may be too important for cutting corners in repairs, but it will forewarn you of the cost.

Once after your initial shopping-around you have settled on a garage, it is not a good idea to chop and change too much. If you can find a garage you trust, and that others also speak well of, it is probably worth sticking to it. A good garage will get to know your car and will watch for problems; for example, it may find a tiny oil leak that is not worth the cost of fixing immediately, but will keep an eye on it in future services.

How to complain

If you are dissatisfied with something the garage has done, don't be fobbed off with excuses. Stand your ground, and insist on seeing the service manager to sort things out. If that doesn't resolve the matter, then insist on talking to the managing director. It is only reasonable to give the garage the chance to put right any complaint before taking it further. But if talking fails, put your grievance in writing to the garage proprietor.

The next line of complaint can be to the manufacturer whose agent the garage is. If you are still convinced you have been given really poor service, you could take your complaint to the local Trading Standards office.

There are also trade and industry organisations to whom you can refer a complaint and seek intervention. They have their own arbitration services to sort out disputes between customer and garage. Keep a note of all the dates and what is said at each stage of the dispute, including any phone calls, and of course keep a record of all correspondence.

These are the relevant addresses you may need:

Society of Motor Manufacturers and Traders (SMMT), Forbes House, Halkin Street, London SWl, tel: 071-235 7000.

Retail Motor Industry Federation (RMIF), 201 Great Portland Street, London Wl, tel: 071-580 9122.

Scottish Motor Trade Association (SMTA), 3 Palmerston Place, Edinburgh, tel: 031-225 3643.

Checking service quality

One worry that many motorists have is whether or not the work for which they are paying has actually been carried out correctly. We are in the hands of our garage, aren't we? We must trust the experts to do what is necessary, and we must pay for it. Not entirely so. It may be extremely difficult for anyone without a jot of mechanical knowledge to check up on how well the servicing has been carried out, but there are things you can do to protect your own interests.

For a start, if you have any reason to suspect that a garage has not satisfactorily completed work for which you have paid, then you could seek the advice of someone who does have sound mechanical knowledge.

Ask the garage to leave in the car for you or your friend's inspection any parts which have to be replaced. If, for example, they fit new spark plugs, insist that the old set is returned to you.

There are a number of simple things you can do for yourself, to check the standard of workmanship to which your car has been subjected. Of course, an inexpert eye will not detect whether or not such jobs as relining brakes have been done efficiently, but you will simply know when you drive that they feel better in operation than they did before.

On the other hand, even the most inexpert person can check some very obvious items. Start by scrutinising the service handbook, to check which items should have been attended to under the service schedule for which your car was booked in. If the service document is not explicit enough, then ask the garage to supply you with a list of the work included in the service. You are the paying customer, so you can call the tune. For example, was checking the battery included in the list? Then re-check it yourself. If a newly serviced car's battery appears to have received no attention, then you might reasonably query whether the rest of the servicing has been satisfactorily attended to.

Did the list include changing the oil? Then pull out the dipstick, and make sure that what is on the end of it is clear, clean looking oil and not sooty-black.

Tyres are often included on a servicing schedule, which may well call for the garage to make a visual inspection and to ensure that the pressures are correct. Check them for yourself.

The windscreen washer level is another mundane item on the average servicing list. Check that the bottle is freshly topped up.

Some of the better garages these days have a window between the service bays and the reception area, so that it is possible to see the work being carried out. If that is the case at the garage you patronise, then make a point of staying for a while to see what happens to your car. Better still, ask if you can talk to the mechanic who actually works on your car, and quiz him on any points you know needed particular attention.

Car 'sympathy'

You may well look after the car well inside and out, but still mistreat it dreadfully. It was made for driving, so how you act at the wheel is a major aspect of care.

Car sympathy is very hard to define, but it is easy to recognise someone who has it, for the smooth and flowing way they drive. It is even easier to spot a driver who lacks any kind of real sympathy for the machine he or she is in control of. The driving style this time is more likely to be staccato, jerky and uncomfortable, punctuated by the occasional scrunched gear change and 'kerbed' tyre.

To drive really well, it is important to care about the effect your inputs on the steering, accelerator, brakes, clutch and gearbox ultimately have on the wear and tear of the car.

Every time you linger on the clutch more than necessary, you are helping to shorten its life. Constantly messing up gear changes puts a strain on the gearbox which could ultimately prove costly. Pulling up the handbrake with a grating sound against the ratchet, instead of troubling to push in the button for a smooth engagement of the brake, is also sloppy and destructive.

Bashing tyres carelessly against the kerb when you park will not only shorten tyre life, but may also put the wheel tracking out of true, leading to an unnecessary bill. It may also knock the balancing weights off the wheels, and cost you money to replace them.

Treat the car as something worth taking care of, and drive it with pride in how smoothly and well you can make it behave. It will last longer, and your passengers will be happier and more comfortable.

Security

Finally, you can treat you car with all the care you would a piece of antique porcelain, but it is all wasted if you make it easy for someone to drive it away. Is your car parked nearby as you read this? Take a look to make sure it is still there. It is just possible that it may have disappeared, becoming one more in the annual statistics of cars which gain the unwelcome attention of thieves.

Autocrime, as the police call it, is a very common occurence. Each year some 1.5 million cars in Britain are stolen or broken into. This means that as a motorist you have a one in ten chance of becoming a victim of autocrime, which now accounts for a quarter of all crime statistics. It is even more common than burglary.

Car theft is also going up all the time, rising steadily year by year. Radios and cassette players in cars are popular prey for thieves, but so are any valuable items left on view inside a car.

What can you do to improve your car's security? Plenty. After all, professional thieves are not the main culprits. Only about one in three car thefts involves a professional. The vast majority involve amateurs – it is generally reckoned that around 70 per cent of all stolen cars are taken by 'joy riders' – in many cases taking advantage of a car door carelessly left unlocked.

There are several simple precautions that can be taken. Nothing will keep out the really determined, skilled criminal, but these will protect you against the far larger number of casual thieves:

➡ Too many motorists are lax about even the most basic security precautions for their cars. Never leave a window or sunroof open, or a door unlocked. It is an open invitation to a potential thief. *Make sure all doors are securely locked.*

➡ Never leave anything of value on show inside the car. Hide away large objects in the boot, and if at all possible carry smaller items with you.

➔ If you do need to stow things in the boot, try to do it in advance, and not just after parking, when your actions may be observed by someone who will then watch you walk away from the car and its contents.

➔ Invest in a security device. Even a simple locking device to clamp between the steering wheel and accelerator pedal can help deter a casual thief.

➔ If you value your car and would really find it inconvenient to have it stolen, consider investing in the cost of a good car alarm system. There is a very wide range of security equipment available for cars, and the more you pay, the greater protection you get. Whether the cost is likely to be worthwhile depends largely on how much the car itself is worth.

➔ Use locking wheel nuts if you live in an area where car owners sometimes wake up in the morning to find their vehicles resting only on piles of bricks, or if your car is equipped with costly and attractive alloy wheels.

➔ Even a tankful of fuel is a temptation to some. If your car does not have one, buy a locking petrol cap.

➔ When you next change your car, go for one with central locking, so there's no chance of leaving any of the doors unlocked by mistake. Consider a good car alarm as well.

Parking for security

➔ Whenever possible, leave the car within sight.

➔ In multi-storey car parks, try to avoid parking near pillars, where a thief could work unobserved.

➔ At night, choose a spot near a street lamp rather than leaving the car in a dark corner.

➔ Avoid regularly leaving your car in places where it is obvious that you will be away for some time: for example, a public car park is better than a cinema car park.

➔ Railway station car parks are notorious for the attention of car thieves who know that most of the vehicles left parked will be there for hours, while their owners are far away at the other end of the rail line.

➔ If you garage your car at night, always lock the garage as well as the car.

Maintaining the bodywork

Never in its life does a car look better than when brand new, glossy and unblemished, before the ravages of traffic, weather, mileage and general neglect take their toll on its appearance.

If only we could all manage to keep our cars permanently in showroom condition, how much more satisfying – and how much safer – it would be. A car's condition invariably seems to play a significant part in the way in which it is driven. A grubby, neglected, corroding car full of rubbish invites sloppy, offhand driving habits. A clean, well-preserved and tidy one, however old, is much more likely to encourage good driving.

Chicken or egg? Do good drivers simply look after their cars better, and bad ones neglect them? Maybe, but ask yourself whether you drive as well as usual at particularly busy times when the car has become a bit scruffy.

Car care is cumulative. Regular care pays dividends in preventing problems from building up. The dirtier a car gets, the harder it is to bring back to pristine condition. The longer a spot of corrosion is left unattended, the bigger the rust patch you will finally face.

Long gone are the days when most car owners were out there on a Sunday morning, brushing and hosing, washing and polishing. But that principle of regular care still holds just as good.

Routine cleaning

As seen in the previous chapter, windows and lights are crucial to safety, so should be cleaned whenever they are at all dirty. The inside of the car should be cleared of any accumulated rubbish after any day's use, and if you smoke, empty and wipe out the ashtray daily to avoid a lingering smell of stale cigarette ends and ash.

Every week treat the car to a more thorough clean. If pressed for time, take it through a car wash, but otherwise wash it thoroughly by hand: you will reach all the hidden parts a mechanical wash never can, and anyway it is good exercise.

Washing

A good shampooing and lashings of clean water does wonders for the bodywork.

Tips for clean washing

➜ Use a proper branded car shampoo, and not a squirt of washing-up liquid, which contains trace elements of salt.

➜ Ensure that the sponge or brush you use is clean and grit-free. A tired, elderly sponge or ragged brush does more harm than good, by putting microscopic scratches onto the paintwork and dulling its shine.

➜ Use plenty of water for rinsing, to sluice away all the residue of dirt and detergent.

The best way to wash a car is the traditional chauffeur's method, starting from the top. That means washing the roof first and working your way down to the wheels, so that the dirtiest parts of the car, nearest to the road, are tackled last.

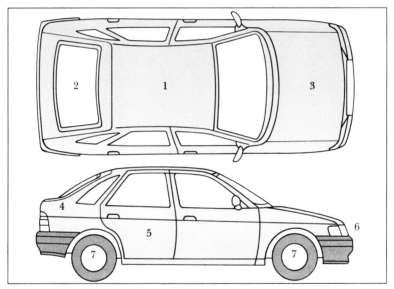

Wash the car in the sequence shown by the numbers.

Change the shampoo water in your bucket several times, so as to avoid replacing the dirt you are washing off with yet more dirt in the washing water. Sluice plenty of clean water over the car to remove all the traces of shampoo: the best way is to use a hose, or several buckets of clean water.

Check that there are no areas where the cleaning has been skimped. If there are, give them extra attention. Don't forget any crevices such as rain gutters, parts of the bodywork below the bumpers and under the door-sills. Pay close attention to the wheels, to clean off the build-up of brake-dust, dirt and grease which tends to accumulate on them. If the wheels are of a particularly fiddly design, an old toothbrush may help in cleaning them.

Dry the paintwork with a clean chamois leather. There is nothing to beat a chamois for making a good, non-smeary job of drying off a car.

Waxing

It is not necessary to polish the bodywork every week, but it should be done at least once every three months, and more often when the weather is persistently bad or the mileage has been unusually high.

After washing the car, leave it at least half an hour before starting polishing, to ensure that the body is completely dry. Polishing the car while it is damp will make it smeary.

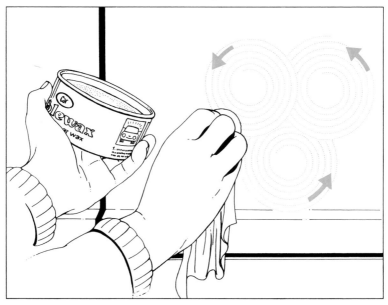

Waxing a car.

Polish should be applied with a soft, clean cloth. Use a good-quality polish, working on a small area at a time applying it in gentle, circular movements.

The traditional car polish is wax, which gives a very good result if you apply it evenly, buff it off carefully, and use it regularly. It can take a bit of effort to apply properly, but it buffs to a good shine and protects the paintwork well. Polymer sealant is easier to apply and lasts longer, but it also tends to be a little more expensive. Use it carefully on dark paintwork, because if not applied properly it can turn streaky. Keep it off any rubber trim, as it may discolour it.

The interior

Vacuum the carpets regularly, ideally once a week, to suck out dirt and grit particles. If allowed to remain in the pile, grit can cut into the carpet and prematurely age it.

Run the vacuum nozzle over the seats and into the door pockets to remove dust and fine debris.

Clean any sticky marks off the upholstery and the trim with a damp cloth, but avoid rubbing too hard and 'fixing' a stain. Clean the rear-view mirror and the insides of the windows with a proprietary glass cleaner. Sunlight tends to leach out chemical deposits from the plastics used in a car's interior, which form a film on the glass, so it is important to clean this off regularly. The problem is compounded if anyone in the car smokes.

Spring cleaning

Every spring take a long, searching look at your car. Despite your good intentions, the cold, wet weather may have stopped you giving it quite the scrupulous care you wanted to. Is its lower bodywork caked in dirt, its upper paintwork dull, the windows less than perfectly clean, the wheels messy, the tyres scuffed? Does it remind you of a weary schoolboy at the end of a long day, trudging home with cap askew, rumpled socks round the ankles and dirty shoes? If so, spring provides a good excuse for getting out into the fresh air to primp and pamper the poor, neglected old car.

Outside first. Start with a thorough bodywork wash, and scrupulously hose out the wheel arches and along the underside of the car to remove any salt deposits left from winter roads. Use a pressure hose at a garage, or a garden hose with water forced out under pressure, for doing the wheel arches.

If it has been an especially harsh winter, with lots of grit and salt on the roads, consider investing in a steam clean for the engine, wheel arches and underside to get rid of all the corrosive residues.

Next, check the bodywork carefully for signs of rust spots, stone chips and paint damage, which should be attended to promptly. Even if you have been doing this regularly, there may be marks that have been hidden by the winter dirt.

If the car is getting old and the paintwork has been badly dulled down by the ravages of winter, it may need 'cutting back' before polishing. That means removing the ingrained dirt and a microscopic amount of the top layer of paint, to get back to clean, pure paint underneath. To do this you need a proprietary cutting agent such as 'T-Cut', which can be highly effective in restoring paintwork if used properly. Follow the instructions on the can carefully, and work on just a small area at a time, using a dry cloth and working in circular patches.

Once the paintwork is clean and bright, it needs protecting. Polish it thoroughly.

If you have any chrome on your car, give it a thorough treat with chrome polish, to restore its shine and remove any superficial surface corrosion.

Wheels can be especially hard to clean up at the end of winter: the best way to tackle them is with lots of sudsy warm water and a suitably shaped brush, plus an old toothbrush for any particularly fiddly bits.

While attending to the exterior of the car, make time to check all the tyres for any cuts, bulges or damage in the sidewalls and for tread wear. This is the time too, to catch up on any checking of the lights you may have missed. Enlist the help of someone in the family or a friend to help see that they are all are functioning correctly and that there are no bulbs which need replacing. Take a close look at the windscreen wiper blades, too. After a hard-working winter, they could well be overdue for replacement.

The first step in spring cleaning inside the car is to remove anything which shouldn't be there. Clear out all the winter's accumulated debris from both the interior and the boot. Next get out all the dirt, grit, dust and mud by giving the floor – boot included – a rigorous vacuuming.

If the seats, trim or headlining look grubby, they can easily be cleaned with a good upholstery cleaner. Cleaners are also available to tackle vinyl trim, but take care to smell any cleaner before you buy. Some are heavily perfumed, and not to everyone's taste.

While clearing out the boot, pay attention to the spare wheel. It may need pumping up: too late to discover it is under-inflated when you have had a puncture and have to put the spare into use.

Winter troubleshooter kit:

In bad weather equip the car with emergency supplies for both it and you:

spade
mat or old piece of carpet (to help with grip under
    slipping wheels)
soft brush or broom (for clearing snow)
screen scraper
de-icer spray
de-icing screen washer additive
booster cables
tow rope
torch
wellington boots
windproof coat
warm sweater
rug
chocolate bars

A car needs a different kind of emergency spares kit in summer from the one you carry (if you're sensible, that is) in winter. Pack away the snow shovel, de-icer, frost scraper and so on for another year, and stock up with self-help items for the summer ahead, such as a large plastic bottle of water for topping up an overheating radiator, a tube of insect bite treatment cream for dealing with the effects of what may fly in through the sunroof, and a screen-cleaning spray and scraper suitable for removing squashed bugs from the windscreen.

Spurred on by all this timely activity, you might just as well take the opportunity to get all the car's affairs in order. Check when the MOT is due, when the road tax needs renewing, when the insurance has to be paid, and when the next service needs to be booked. Finally, don't forget all those other things you should be checking anyway, like oil and coolant levels, the state of the battery and the fluid in the screen wash.

If you have been thinking about changing your car, spring is a good time to do it. The car market revives again after the sluggish winter months, and with your car newly cossetted it will look as though it is worth more than it did when it was dirty.

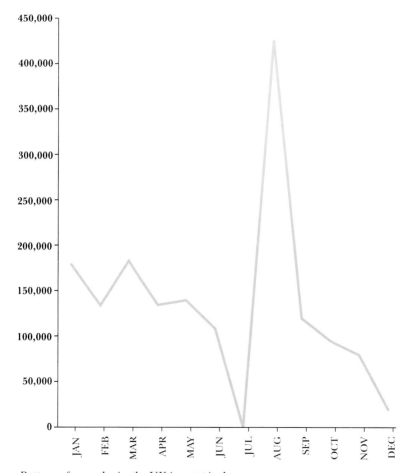

Pattern of car sales in the UK in a typical year.

Valeting

Paying to have a car professionally valeted is a costly business, but the results can be remarkable, restoring a tired and dreary looking car to showroom condition. It is possible to achieve the same results with a do-it-yourself job, but is time-consuming and hard work. Nevertheless, it can be well worth the effort.

The valet service

Professional valeting of a car will involve the following jobs:

➜ thorough bodywork wash and dry

➜ removal of ingrained dirt from paint

➜ paint polished and buffed to shine

➜ chrome polished, plastic bumpers treated with restorer

➜ engine steam-cleaned

➜ wheels cleaned

➜ interior vacuumed

➜ all windows cleaned inside and out

➜ upholstery and trim cleaned

Valeting is basically giving the car the equivalent of a very good spring clean, with a few extra tricks thrown in. A proprietary plastics and vinyl cleaner used on interior surfaces can buff them back to a gleaming sheen. Putting extra effort into cleaning any trim is well rewarded with the extra shine it adds to the car's appearance. Cleaning polypropylene bumpers with a proprietary restorer will overcome dullness and fading.

For a real showroom look, treat the tyres to a coat of tyre black. It is the final touch which puts a valeted car in a class apart from a merely clean one.

Under cover

Cars, like people, benefit from a bit of protection. A car left out in the cold and damp at night is an invitation to rust and the attention of thieves. A car under cover stays in better shape.

The best place for a car to spend its nights – and its days, when not being used, and especially when the weather is wet – is in a safe, securely locked garage.

The problem is, in the same way as many people are pretty cavalier about the way they look after their cars, so plenty of people are just as careless about how well they look after the garages in which they put them.

It is not really good enough to drive the car into the garage and slam the door. In fact, if the car has been out in the rain and is still wet, and the garage is warm and poorly ventilated, then tucking up your moist machinery in a well-sealed garage is one of the worst things you can do to it. Leaving it out in the rain would be kinder. If you wanted to encourage a piece of metal to rust as quickly as possible, then how would you go about it? Immerse it in water, and put it into a warm, moist atmosphere to encourage the damp to start corroding the metal. Put a wet car in a warm, airless garage, and you are creating precisely the same environment.

So, to make a garage a healthy enviroment for storing a car, it must be well ventilated, with a good passage of air to prevent damp from turning to condensation. But while airflow is important, any windows or airvents left open should be away from the prevailing wind, so that rain cannot be driven in. Neither does this mean leaving a door open, which is only an invitation to thieves. Any leaks or damage to the fabric of the garage should be attended to promptly. In particular, the roof ought to be kept in good order, with no tiles missing or any places where rain can get in. A steady dribble of water on to the bodywork through a hole in the garage roof is very bad news for a car's state of health.

A badly maintained and untidy garage is a hazardous place for a car.

It is not only damp and car thieves which are potential hazards to the car in its own garage. What about the other things with which it has to share its living space? It should have plenty of room all around it, not be squashed in amongst all the assorted paraphernalia of family life. A garage groaning with rubbish is a hazardous place for a car to be stored. Even useful items, like bicycles, lawn mowers or pots of paint, are perilous neighbours for the pristine paintwork of a manoeuvring car.

It is wise to cushion any likely trouble-spots where car and garage might come into unwanted contact. Where the doors open, pad the wall or any protrusions with something to soften the impact if a door is flung wide carelessly at some time. An old cushion or discarded mattress is ideal. If garden tools are by necessity stowed in the garage, make sure thay cannot fall or be knocked onto the car bodywork by accident. A toppled hoe could mean a costly repair.

If the car has a tendency to drop oil when it is parked for a while, put a tray of sand on the floor under the engine to catch the drops and keep the floor clean and free from dangerous oil, which can be hazardous under foot.

Protection from the weather

If you do not have a garage, there are still ways you can protect your car from the worst ravages of inclement weather.

➡ Park it where it has some measure of protection from wind and rain – sheltered by the side of a house, for example.

➡ Park with the bonnet away from the prevailing wind, to avoid cold draughts from being blown into the engine, and making the car vulnerable to starting problems.

➡ Keep the car bodywork regularly cleaned and well waxed, to give it the means of shrugging off insidious bad weather.

➡ Check regularly that drain-holes, designed to let rainwater flow away and not become trapped in body box sections, are kept clear of debris or fallen leaves.

Corrosion

Rust is the big enemy of car ownership. It eats into the bodywork and into the value of your car, and should always be dealt with swiftly, as soon as it appears. Putting off a rust repair always means facing a bigger job when you do finally get around to it.

There are two ways in which rust attacks a car. The most troublesome type of corrosion starts from the inside, triggered by water getting at panels where the moisture has been able to linger and start eating into the metal unseen. The front and rear wings are common starting points for rust, because water and mud flung upwards by the wheels tends to cling and hold the moisture in place.

That is a good reason for regularly hosing out the wheel arches, to ensure they are kept clean, and for diligently checking for water leaks anywhere else around the car.

The second way in which rust starts attacking a car is from the outside in, triggered by surface damage to the paintwork. This may be due to stones flung up and chipping the paint, breaking its surface and allowing water to seep underneath. It may also be caused by scuffing or minor accident damage which is left unattended.

If you are too short of time to treat the damage promptly, always take action at least to stop the rot by treating the exposed metal with rust inhibitor, and then take more extensive measures as soon as you can.

Treating minor rust

As part of your regular inspection of the bodywork pay special attention to the edges of the wheel arches, the front edge of the bonnet, the section of body below the front bumper, the lower edges of the doors, the door sills, the boot lip or bottom edge of the tailgate. Those are the places where rust tends to appear first.

Any tiny stone chips, where the paint surface is broken but the primer is still intact, can be rectified simply with touch-up paint to match the bodywork colour. After treating an area of chipping and giving it time to dry completely, be sure to give it a coat of polish to protect it.

Chips or scratches which have gone through to bare metal need treatment with a rust stabiliser and inhibitor. Follow the instructions supplied with it, and once the area is properly stabilised and protected, paint it with primer and body colour top coat.

Patching holes

Rust holes in the bodywork are bad news. Ideally things should never have been allowed to get that far, and treating rust at the first sign of its erupting keeps it at bay.

If you do find holes which need treatment, or perhaps have bought a 'bargain' second-hand car with some rust in need of attention, first decide whether the job of repairing it is one you can cope with. Rust in important structural areas of the car may be best left to a garage. Your next MOT certificate may depend on the quality of the repair, and it makes no sense to bodge a job and then spend even more on having it put right than a professional repair would have cost you in the first place.

If you plan to do the job yourself, do not be tempted to squeeze it in as an extra task when you are rushed. Car body repairs need time and thoroughness. A hurried job will probably end up looking like it.

Start by removing all signs of rust and flaked paint from the edges of the hole, using an electric sander or coarse wet-and-dry paper. When the rust has gone you will be left with sharp edges. Trim away any weak, thin metal with cutters to leave a clean, healthy edge. Next, flatten the edges using a small hammer to dish them slightly below the level of the surrounding bodywork. The edges now need treating with rust inhibitor to stop rust spreading any further. If possible, get the inhibitor on to the metal under the edges of the hole.

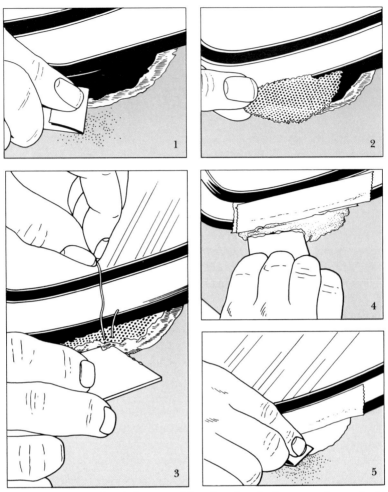

Filling a hole. 1, Sand down and key the edge. 2, Insert a wire mesh. 3, Apply filler from edge. 4, Build up the filler to seal the hole, protecting the paintwork with adhesive tape. 5, Rub the filler down to a smooth surface.

Now the hole needs to be bridged, ready to take the filler which will cover it. A piece of wire mesh, which comes with a body repair kit, should be cut to a shape slightly larger than the actual hole.

Use small amounts of filler all round the edge to hold the mesh in place. Once it has hardened enough to keep it there, you can carry on with the job of filling in over the mesh. Build up the filler so that it comes slightly higher than the surface level of bodywork around what used to be the hole. Then, when dry, you can rub it down first with coarse and then with fine abrasive paper until the surface is smooth right across the repair.

Finally, when the surface is as smooth and flat as possible, it is ready to be primed and then painted.

Larger holes can be a problem, and are more easily dealt with using glass-fibre mesh, resin and hardener. The repair job is basically similar to the method involving wire mesh, and the instructions with the glass-fibre body repair kit will tell you how to mix the resin and hardener.

Dealing with dents

Large dents are hard for an amateur to fix, and are best entrusted to a garage or body repair shop. They can sometimes be repaired, but more often it is simpler, cheaper and better-looking to replace the panel or a section of it.

Smaller dents still spoil the look of a car and can be rectified more easily. If the dent is in a piece of bodywork where you can get to the back of it, try to push it out with your hand, or using a small hammer tap gently against a cushioning layer of soft cloth held against the underside of the dent.

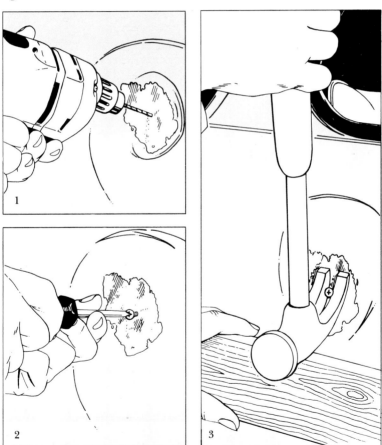

1, Drill a hole in the middle of the dent. 2, Insert a screw. 3, Prise out the dent with the screw and pliers or a claw hammer

Another way of tackling the dent, which may be helpful in areas where you cannot reach the back, is to drill a small hole through the deepest part nearest the centre, and then try to pull it out. Do this by inserting a self-tapping screw into the hole and screwing it part way in, and then use pliers or mole grips to spring the dent outwards.

If that does not work, use a claw-headed hammer, hooked behind the screw, to try to prise the dent outwards. If successful, you will need to rustproof the edges of the holes thoroughly, then fill, prime and paint them.

If some of the damaged area is left partly indented, it may need treating with filler. 'Key' the area first with fine abrasive paper to slightly roughen it, so that the filler will hold. Then fill, prime and paint as described earlier.

The MOT test

The name 'MOT' for the annual health check for cars is a misnomer. It has been a considerable time since the Ministry of Transport has been responsible for administering the test, but the name has stuck and has refused to yield to the arrival of the Department of Transport.

The purpose of the test is to ensure that the car is in a reasonable state of health and road worthiness, and effectively to outlaw elderly bangers which are poorly maintained and may potentially endanger other road users. The test takes about half an hour and is a good general guide to a car's condition.

The MOT test should not really be anything to worry about. It need not be a major trauma if you have kept the car regularly serviced and been scrupulous about staying up to date with regular routine maintenance.

All the same, it seems inevitable that a car which has been running perfectly well all year suddenly seems to develop an ominous squeak from the suspension, a limp feel to the brakes or a sudden nerve-wracking steering wobble just as the MOT becomes due.

As the time for the MOT test comes round again, it is conscience time for many motorists. When did you last look closely at your windscreen wipers, or examine your tyres, or check your lights, or scrutinise the webbing of your seat-belts? Not very recently, if you are like the majority of drivers, who seem to find such mundane items easy to ignore for months on end. However, those are the kind of niggling little items that can so easily catch you out on the MOT test.

Even if the car has been recently serviced, and you are perfectly happy with the condition of the brakes, steering and so on, there are still a number of other potential causes of failure – for example, seat belts, wipers, tyres, indicator lights, horn, wheels and exhaust system. Paying a garage to check such items which you can easily do yourself, if you know what to look for, is an expensive luxury. Run through a checklist of potential failure points well in advance of when the next MOT is due, and leave yourself plenty of time to have any problems put right.

If more motorists checked out their cars as an annual pre-MOT routine, there would be fewer failures. It is a sad indictment of the general condition of older cars on our roads that every year more than four million cars in Britain fail their MOT.

Items to check

Give the car a thorough check for items which you may be able to put right. However, if the brakes seem spongy, the steering feels sloppy or there is evidence of creeping rust which may be a structural hazard, have the car seen to by a garage.

Lights

Ensure that all the lights are in working order, with no bulbs blown and the headlamp dipping is correctly adjusted and working properly.

Check for pale or damaged red covers on the rear lights. Reflectors must be in sound condition. Reflective tape is not acceptable as a substitute.

The indicators should flash at a pulse rate of between 60 and 120 flashes a minute. It is an easy thing to check yourself: use a watch with a second-hand to check that the indicators flash between five and ten times every five seconds. The flashing light on the dashboard must work, too.

Steering, suspension

Excessive play in the steering can fail the test. If the car has power steering, it must be working satisfactorily. There should be no leaks or damage in the suspension. Check for worn shock absorbers, a common cause of MOT failure. Press down on each corner of the car in turn and it should spring firmly back up with one rebound. If it rebounds several times or feels soggy then the shock absorbers need replacing.

Brakes

Braking efficiency is a crucial part of the test and is checked on a brake test apparatus. If you have any doubts about the car's brakes, have them attended to before the test.

As well as the footbrakes what about the hand brake – does it hold the car? It is a test item. Check it by parking on a steep hill and ensuring that the car does not creep with the gears in neutral and just the handbrake engaged.

Tyres

There should be an absolute minimum of 1.6 mm of tread, around the entire circumference of the tyre and across at least three quarters of its width. Check it by inserting a 10p piece end-on into the tread. There should be enough rubber protruding to hide the serrated edge of the coin and almost to touch the writing round the coin.

Any cuts or bulges in the tyre sidewalls are failure points. Look carefully at the walls of all the tyres, including the spare, on both sides. In the test the car will be put up on a ramp for the tester to examine them.

The wheels will be examined too. Any serious buckling or other damage to the wheel rim is a failure point, although a small nick in the metal usually is not.

Seatbelts

Worn or damaged seatbelts can make a car fail the MOT, yet most drivers never give them a second thought. What you must check for is any fraying at the edges of the webbing, or signs of the fibres stretching, or the reel mechanism sticking.

A small amount of surface 'balling' on older belts, through years of friction, is no cause for alarm unless the fibres are actually broken. But if the strands have split or been cut in some way, they will not pass the test.

Belts can become stretched if the car has been in a crash at some time, after which – having done their job – they should have been replaced.

A very common cause of damage to belt webbing is the careless habit of shutting the car door on a trailing seat-belt, or trampling it under-foot. Another cause of damage is exposure to corrosives such as antifreeze which eat away the webbing.

Chassis

Severe rust eating into the floorpan of the car or weakening its structural frame is potentially serious, will certainly fail the car, and is likely to be expensive to put right.

Never ignore signs of rust developing; always treat corrosion promptly to prevent its spreading, and if it is in crucial structural areas consult a garage before putting the car in for the test.

Exhaust

How about that long, ugly, eminently forgettable thing underneath the car, the exhaust pipe: does it rattle, or make a spluttering sound as you drive? If so, it may be loose or leaking. Either fault can fail the car, not to mention what it may do to you if fumes start seeping into the car's interior. An elderly and infirm exhaust pipe should be repaired or relaced.

General items

Under the MOT regulations, wipers must be in good working order, set correctly and clear the glass efficiently. If they flop off the edge of the screen, or if the blades are ragged with trailing slivers of rubber, the car will fail.

If you have been lucky enough not to use them for a while because of dry weather, you may not have noticed any of the tell-tale signs that the blades were becoming worn, such as smearing on the screen.

Examine them closely for splits just behind the wiping edge, where the rubber is thinnest. If you are in any doubt about the blades, replace them anyway – it won't cost you very much.

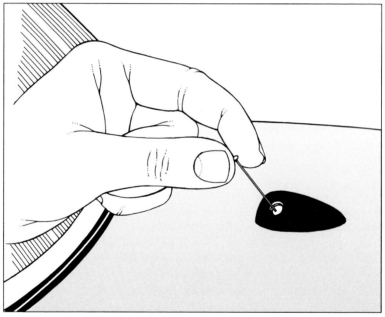

Adjusting a washer jet. Insert the pointed end of a pin into the jet and use it to adjust the direction of water squirted out.

We have all seen cars with windscreen washers so badly awry that they shower the scenery or the roof with water instead of squirting on to the screen. They won't get through the MOT, which demands an adequate flow of water on to the screen. Re-directing rogue jets is a very simple task: gently tweak them back in the right direction with a pin inserted into the washer hole. But if the washer can manage no more than a feeble burble of water, it is probably best left to a garage to sort it out.

According to the test regulations, the car's horn must work well enough to give, in the tester's judgement, 'sufficient audible warning'. It must also sound immediately you press the button. If it doesn't, or just gives a faint squeak, it needs fixing.

Pre-test checklist

This is the check-list the test examiner follows, covering all the items which form part of the test.

Lighting equipment
  front and rear lamps
  headlamps
  headlamp aim
  stop lamps
  rear reflectors
  direction indicators

Steering and suspension
  steering control
  steering mechanism/system
  power steering
  transmission shafts
  wheel bearings
  front suspension
  rear suspension
  shock absorbers
  wheel alignment

Brakes
  controls
  condition of service brake system
  condition of parking brake system
  service brake performance
  parking brake peformance

Tyres and wheels
  tyre type
  tyre condition
  road wheels

Seatbelts
  mountings
  condition
  operation

General
  windscreen wipers and washers
  horn
  exhaust system
  exhaust emissions
  vehicle structure

Emission test

Regulations brought into effect in November 1991 extended the MOT test to include exhaust emissions. This is not something you can easily check yourself, but it is a simple enough task to have it done as many garage forecourts are now installing gas analyser equipment to check car exhausts.

An engine which is kept properly tuned should give no cause for fear under the emissions test, but if your engine is allowed to go off tune you could have a problem.

On the road

To hear some people talking you would think that all the best days of motoring were long since past. In some ways, perhaps they are: as a child, avidly watching the road ahead over my father's shoulder, I remember fewer cars, more courtesy from other drivers, and a real sense of adventure when embarking on a long journey. However, I also recall the times when the radiator boiled, the way our family car struggled to climb the Devon hills, and the frequency with which it had to be serviced. Cars today are so much more reliable, sail up hills without a qualm, and, thank heaven, need servicing much less often.

But it is true that the roads are now much more congested, and we should all drive accordingly. Unfortunately, the frustration of crawling along in traffic tends to rev up some drivers' tempers, and make them aggressive and more prone to taking chances. Intelligent driving, on the other hand, often needs restraint, common sense, care, planning and a modicum of humour. Be flexible enough to handle any situation as it arises, calmly, maturely and without being pushy.

Town driving

Driving in urban traffic takes patience and strong concentration. Let your mind stray for a moment, and you can suddenly find yourself impaled on the back bumper of the car in front, or even worse, in collision with a pedestrian.

There are so many distractions in towns and cities that you cannot depend on other people concentrating on where they are going. Pedestrians, cyclists, motorcyclists and drivers are all at risk of being affected by 'visual pollution', meaning too many other things to look at besides what is happening on the road.

Town driving can be very frustrating, but it is vital to keep calm, curb your impatience, and make allowances for other road-users' mistakes and stupidities. In situations where traffic is getting knotted up, it does not help to drive right up to another vehicle and engage in an orgy of horn-blowing and fist shaking. Give others room to sort themselves out, and try to avoid aggravating any problem.

Watch out for pedestrians, who may not always be looking where they are going, and expect them to do the unexpected. Make extra allowances for elderly people who cannot always move quickly, and for young children who may move much too quickly and unpredictably.

Pedestrians have precedence on marked crossings: legally, traffic must stop for them. Be ready, therefore, to stop whenever approaching a Zebra crossing, and at Pelican crossings controlled by traffic lights, remember that you may only drive across them at a flashing amber light when there is no pedestrian on the crossing.

When approaching traffic lights controlling junctions, think ahead and plan which lane you want to be in. If you want to turn right, signal early to give other vehicles the chance to manoeuvre around you.

At junctions with criss-cross yellow 'box' markings on the road surface, the law says you may not enter the box unless your exit is clear; treat all junctions as if they had yellow boxes to avoid blocking other traffic if the lights change while you are stationary in the centre of the junction.

Keep a careful look-out for motorcyclists and cyclists, who may be tempted to weave in and out of traffic to make progress through the jams, and who often pull rather sharply out of side turnings. Especially watch out for them when you are leaving a parked car; drivers often only seem to look out for large vehicles before opening an offside door.

Be especially careful near bus stops, where people may hurry off the bus and step incautiously out in front of traffic, and where people running to catch the bus are also a hazard. Beware of the bus driver trying to make up his schedule, who may pull out rather sharply in front of you.

Look out for one-way streets. In busy traffic and an unfamiliar town, especially where large vehicles are parked blocking the view of a crucial sign, it is easy to make the mistake of turning into a road which is designated one-way, and driving the wrong way down it. Parked cars all facing in the same direction are a sure sign.

Unfamiliar mini-roundabouts can be tricky. Treat them in the same way as a large roundabout, and always give way to traffic on your right. If in any doubt about whose right of way it is, err on the side of caution and hold back.

Bus lanes can get you into trouble. It is an offence to drive in a bus lane at the times specified for the exclusive use of buses, taxis and cycles. Resist the temptation to use it as a short cut at those times, or you risk prosecution. At other times – and they vary greatly from one bus lane to another, but are generally geared away from rush-hours – the lane is open to all traffic.

Take care where you park. Never stop on the zig-zag markings on the approach to a pedestrian crossing, or within 15 feet of a junction. Do not stop, even briefly, overlapping the pavement. It is very hazardous to poorly sighted people.

Parking tickets are one of the irritating hazards of town driving. If you want to avoid them, never park without checking the waiting signs, and in street car parks check for pay-and-display dispensers.

Saying you did not know you were supposed to pay is no excuse, and will not let you off a ticket.

Parking

Being able to position and leave the car efficiently is pretty crucial to driving, but many people seem to be clueless about parking and incapable of manoeuvring their cars skilfully in a confined space. This is probably because until recently parking was not part of the driving test. Now that candidates are required to demonstrate that they know how to parallel-park a car at the kerbside, standards should improve, but that's too late for offending existing drivers.

If you are one of those people who hates having to negotiate the car into a parking space, take heart. Like anything else in life, patience and practice pay off, and parking is a technique that can be learned.

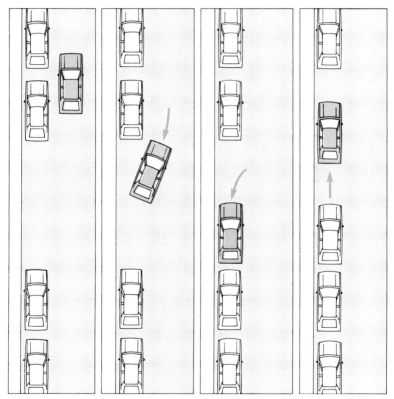

How to park in a space between cars at the kerbside.

The key to it is always to reverse into a gap. Do not be tempted to try to drive forwards to park between cars at the kerbside, as this is much harder. When looking for a kerbside parking space, try to find a gap at least one and a half times the length of your car. Drive just past it until your back bumper is about level with the middle of the parked car ahead of your spot (1). Check your mirrors, look over your shoulder, and start reversing parallel with the other vehicle until your rear bumpers are level. Then start pulling on left lock to turn your tail end into the gap, looking over your shoulder and towards the far inner corner of the parking space as you do so (2).

Continue edging backwards until you are angled into the gap, with the back of your car pointing towards the kerb and the front end positioned diagonally outwards. Next start swinging the steering wheel hard in the opposite direction. Take care at this point to keep glancing to your front nearside corner as you swing into the gap, to avoid letting it accidentally clip the back offside corner of the car you're parking behind.

Carry on edging backwards on hard right lock until your car is close to the one behind, and is also nearly parallel with the kerb (3). Now edge forwards, straightening up as you go (4). Manoeuvre gently to bring the car midway between the two others, and as close as possible to the kerb without actually allowing the wheels to touch it. This can be tricky, but it is important to avoid this 'kerbing' all the same. You'll know if you've failed in this respect by the squeal of complaining rubber.

If after plenty of practice you still find yourself lacking the knack, you're not alone: it does not come naturally to everyone. Rather than leaving it as a blind science and a daily embarrassment, it might be worth contacting a reputable local driving school and booking a single lesson in order to learn just this.

Alternatively, a friend or relative might be able to show you how to do it, or you could practise with a couple of friends whose parking is as shaming as yours. Persuade them to go with you to an empty car park one Sunday morning, and then two of you take it in turn playing 'bookends' with your cars, while the third one of the trio practises parking between the other two. If you do this, taking away the stress of a busy street where you usually attempt to park, you might well find that the knack will suddenly click into place.

Country driving

Driving is at its most pleasurable out on the open road, in glorious countryside. That is where you can enjoy your car while relishing the scenery. However, it does not mean that driving on country roads is any less demanding than elsewhere. The countryside has its own hazards, albeit quite different from those in town.

Some country roads have rough, broken surfaces and potholes, especially minor roads that get little attention. Others, especially in wet weather, are slippery from mud deposited on them by agricultural vehicles going about their business. Treat either with caution.

Be prepared for very large farm vehicles to loom up in the road ahead, particularly in summer when combine harvesters and heavily laden hay lorries are on the move. When overtaking such vehicles, make allowances for their length, ponderous steering and the hazard of showers of loose straw which may fly off them. You may require extra patience as country roads are often narrow and bendy, and you may have to stare at the lumbering bale of hay for several minutes until you find a stretch of road suitable for overtaking.

Country roads create their own problems, such as slow-moving vehicles and animals. Use landscape and other features, such as the line of telegraph poles, to anticipate the road ahead.

Animals represent a common hazard. Sheep and cattle grazing freely at the edges of unfenced moorland roads can be unpredictable, and you should always drive past them at a speed which permits you to stop in time if one of them suddenly darts out.

Always drive round corners expecting a flock of sheep or herd of cows to be just the other side of the bend, with your speed moderated accordingly. If you do find them there, stop and resist the temptation to sound your horn. Give whoever is attending them the chance to move them on without harrassment.

Horses being ridden along country lanes should be treated with respect and caution. Even a well-schooled horse or pony under the control of a good, skilled rider can shy sideways at the approach of a car. Slow right down, being prepared to stop if necessary, and give them as wide a berth as possible as you drive slowly by. Do not then put your foot hard down again the moment you are past, as the noise of a revving car engine might frighten the horse.

Use the scenery to guide your driving. On twisty country roads, for example, watch out for the direction of a line of roadside trees or telegraph poles to warn of which way the road is turning.

Make allowances for the variations in country roads. Fast crosscountry stretches are often interspersed with small villages, where it is important to slow right down and make allowances for pedestrians strolling across the road and local delivery vehicles in no particular hurry. Some motorists cannot resist continuing at speed through villages, but it is dangerous and anti-social, as well as illegal, to do so.

If you drive on a remote country lane with gates, always close them behind you, even if you found them open, and if you have to cross a ford, drive through it slowly and steadily, then test the brakes before driving on.

Motorway driving

Motorways are statistically the safest type of road. Despite the impression created by newspaper headlines about motorway pile-ups, they suffer fewer accidents per mile than any other kind of road. But because of the consistently higher speeds at which traffic on motorways moves, any small error risks more serious consequences than on ordinary roads.

That is a very good reason for ensuring that you do not let your attention wander. Motorway driving can be tiring, so the rule-of-thumb about stopping for a breather every couple of hours on a long journey is especially important. Most motorways are reasonably well endowed with service areas where you can take a reviving snack or coffee, or merely stretch your legs.

Because of the comfortable, cocooning effect of a modern car thrumming along at a steady speed, it is all too easy to let the needle creep up the speedo without noticing how fast you are actually going. Keep an eye on the clock.

The combination of driving too fast and too close is potentially lethal, and the commonest cause of motorway pile-ups. Maintain a sensible distance behind the vehicle in front, and never be tempted to close up if another, slower driver fails to move over.

Lane discipline and overtaking

It is just as vital to keep a good look about you, making frequent use of all the mirrors so that you know what other vehicles are doing behind and beside you, as well as ahead. Always double-check before changing lanes.

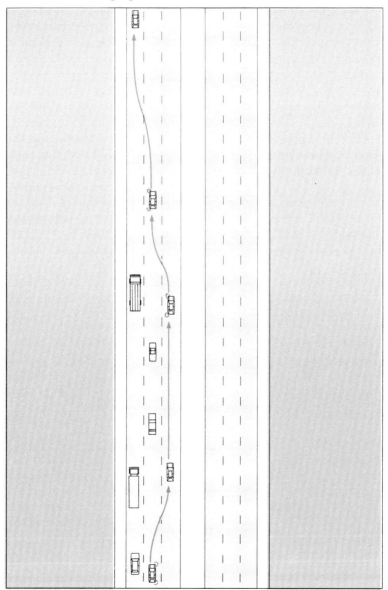

Overtaking on a motorway.

Many drivers are very careless about lane discipline. Firmly suppress the common misconception that there are 'fast' lanes on a motorway. Anything other than the left-hand lane is an 'overtaking' lane, but despite constant advice from the Department of Transport, drivers clog the middle and right-hand lanes. British law dictates that you may only overtake on the right, and that having overtaken you should pull in again to the furthest lane on left that allows you a reasonably clear road ahead.

Always give other drivers ample notice of your intentions, and allow at least as long in time for them to register your signals as you would on an ordinary road. It is wrong, and dangerous, to signal at the last moment as you are pulling out. The same applies when moving back into your original lane again after overtaking: do so gradually, checking in both driving and wing mirrors, and ensuring that you give clear advance warnings to other motorway users.

Whenever preparing to overtake, pay particular attention to the danger of failing to notice another vehicle in your car's blind spot. This falls in the area just to the rear of the car, between the coverage of the interior driving mirror and the door mirror. Regular checking in the mirror should keep you informed of the road behind, and hence alerted to any car coming up behind that has suddenly 'disappeared'.

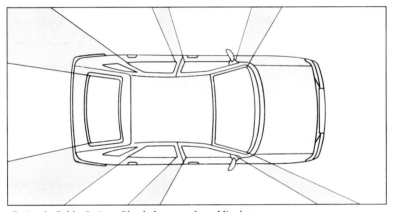

Driver's field of view. Shaded areas show blind spots

Take special care about overtaking on a motorway on windy days, especially when passing heavy trucks. A sudden gust of wind as you pass the front of the lorry can whip your car sharply sideways. Drive in the centre of the lane you are in, to give the widest berth between your vehicle and others on either side.

Entering and leaving motorways

The hard shoulder is only for emergencies such as a disabling car fault or illness. It is never to be used for picnic stops, for stretching the legs, stopping to combat a bout of tiredness, or for 'comfort' breaks.

If you do have to stop on the hard shoulder, always get all passengers out of the car, through the doors on the side away from the traffic, and up to the top of the motorway embankment. Then they are safe from injury if another vehicle should slew off the road and hit your parked car – as has been known to happen.

As a matter of courtesy and consideration to drivers trying to join the motorway, always pay special attention at points where slip roads are feeding into the carriageway. If a vehicle is approaching on the slip road, and there is room to do so, move out into the middle lane to give him space to join the nearside lane without hindrance or having to reduce his speed.

When you are joining a motorway, watch for a suitable gap in the traffic flow, increase your speed to roughly that of the traffic in the nearside lane, check the mirrors, signal that you intend to join the motorway, and pull out into the left-hand lane.

When leaving the motorway, watch for the signs which warn you of the exit a mile ahead, then half a mile, and then those that show that the exit is imminent at 300, 200 and 100 yards (three, two and one diagonal line). Move into the nearside lane well ahead, and use your left-hand indicator to let other traffic know you are pulling off.

Switching lanes suddenly, or swerving violently across several lanes of traffic at the last minute, is extremely dangerous. If you fail to notice a turn-off until the last moment, don't take a chance on trying to make it, but instead drive on to the next junction and turn back on the other side of the motorway to return to the exit you wanted.

Motorways at night

Night driving on motorways has extra hazards and responsibilities. As on all other roads, but even more important at motorway speeds, only ever drive at the speed which enables you to stop in the distance you can see ahead in your headlamps.

When it is misty, resist the temptation to switch to full-beam, because the light will bounce back at you off the fog, and make it harder to see forward. Dipped beam is safer. Beware of rolling banks of fog which can suddenly engulf the road. This applies to any road, but on motorways special care is needed as too often drivers are tempted to drive too fast and then cannot brake in time if there is a hazard or a stationary vehicle ahead.

Fatigue is an extra risk at night too, and hard-hearted though it may seem, the law will penalise you if you stop for a quick kip on the hard shoulder. At the first sign of sleepiness, slow down and increase the ventilation in the car: switch off the heater, direct a flow of air on to your face, and open a window if necessary. Then pull off the motorway at the first opportunity. Long distances on a motorway can be tedious, so it can help to have something in the car to keep your mind alert, such as a conversation with a passenger, a tape player or a radio. A talk programme is more likely to stimulate and keep you awake than a soothing late night music channel, which can have a perilously lulling effect in a cossetting, warm car.

Contraflows

Contraflows are the bane of driving life on modern motorways. Treat them as you would any other hazardous obstacle in the road ahead, with caution and care, and by slowing down. Most of them are clearly signed. Stay alert, watch out for sudden switches to the other carriageway in a tunnel of cones, and keep to a sensible speed.

Fuel consumption

One potential problem many drivers overlook on motorways is that of using fuel faster than on normal roads, due to the much higher cruising speeds. Keep an eye on the fuel gauge. AA and RAC patrols bear witness to how often drivers run out of petrol on the motorway. Err on the side of caution, rather than gambling on being able to get to the next service area beyond the one coming up.

Basic motorway law

There are specific rules governing the use of motorways. This is a summary of them:

➡ No stopping except in an emergency.

➡ No L-drivers, pedestrians, cyclists, horses or motorcycles under 50 cc.

➡ Drive on the left except when overtaking.

➡ Maximum speed 70 mph.

➡ No heavy goods vehicles in the right hand lane of 3-lane carriageways.

➡ No U-turns.

Road signs

Advance information about hazards ahead is provided by road signs. Most of them are in one of three shapes: triangle, circle or rectangle. A triangle with a red edge is a warning sign. A circle with a red edge tells you of something which is prohibited. A circle with a blue background gives you an instruction. Rectangular signs contain information.

From left to right: roundabout, no entry, lane instructions.

Road signs are intended to help you plan your driving ahead in the safest manner, to protect you from arriving unexpectedly at a potential hazard, and to help guide you with route directions.

We all gen up on road signs for the driving test, and then pay scant attention to memorising them thereafter. But they merit greater interest than that, so if your knowledge is hazy, buy a copy of the Highway Code and give yourself a refresher.

Do you need it? See how many of these you recognise:

Do you know these? See p.135 to check.

Driving in different conditions

Driving is a constantly changing skill. The time of day, the seasons, weather conditions and some of the things we add to our cars such as roofracks and trailers all play a part in the way in which we drive, the way the car behaves and the hazards we face.

As my driving instructor was fond of saying: 'Engage brain before engaging gear.' A wise driver pays careful attention to the factors that may have an effect on driving conditions. The key to coping safely with these is to 'read' the road ahead, and anticipate problems before having to tackle them.

Night driving

If your eyesight is sound and your car's lights are in good condition, night driving should not present any particular problem. If in any doubt about your eyesight, have it tested.

Keep the car's windows thoroughly clean, because dirty or scratched glass both restricts your vision, causes distractions and creates dazzle from night lighting and oncoming headlights.

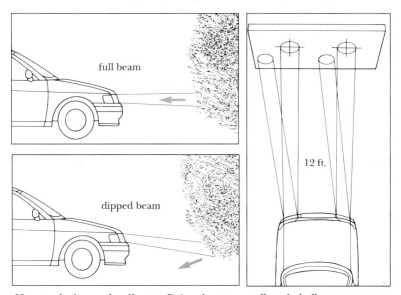

How to check your headlamps. Drive close to a wall and chalk two crosses on the wall exactly in line with and the same height as the centre of the headlights. Reverse straight back till you are 12 ft away from the wall. When on full beam the lights should cover the crosses, dipped they should be lower and to the left.

Switch on dipped headlamps as soon as daylight starts to fade, and take extra care at dusk, when other vehicles become more difficult to see if their drivers do not switch their lights on promptly.

When using full-beam headlamps for driving outside urban areas, be constantly at the ready to switch to dip when another car approaches. We have all experienced the annoyance and danger of being dazzled. Check your own lights regularly to see that they are properly dipped when they are meant to be.

Carry a torch in the car at night for use in any emergency. Remember to switch off the lights when parking the car, except when parking on a main road, with a 30 mph (or less) speed limit and facing the oncoming traffic, in which case the sidelights must be left on. However, you must not leave a car long in these circumstances as a few hours of the sidelights will drain the battery. Remember in particular to turn off sidelights if you have put them on for only gloomy conditions – it is easy to walk away from the car forgetting that the lights are on if it is not actually dark.

Hazardous weather

Our fickle and often inclement climate throws all kinds of weather hazards in our path. Most of the accidents that occur in bad weather are primarily due to drivers going too fast for the conditions.

Slow down and take extra care when the weather turns foul. Never forget that it is better to arrive late than not at all. It may sound odd to say this, but it does help if you try to relax when you're driving in bad weather. If you're too tense, and grip the steering wheel so tightly that your knuckles turn white, while your back gives a passable impression of a telegraph pole, you could be in for problems. A tense grip on the steering makes you less sensitive to the feel of it, and less likely to notice the moment when the wheels do start to lose their grip.

Don't let yourself be hassled by other drivers emulating Nigel Mansell, and wanting you to go faster than you feel is safe. Let your own judgement alone dictate your speed when the going is tricky, and do not be influenced by anyone else.

Rain

Very heavy rain can cut down visibility considerably and can make the road surface as slippery as ice. Put on dipped headlamps, and use foglights if it is hard to see ahead. Slow right down.

Wind

The faster you are travelling, the more wind can affect you and put the car in danger of being blown off course. Cut your speed and watch out for other vehicles deviating from their lane. Try to stay well clear of high-sided vehicles, which can be blown over in strong winds, and be ultra-cautious if you have to overtake one.

Fog

Fog is one of the most frightening weather hazards. Slow right down to a speed at which you can stop within the length of road you can see ahead. Switch on dipped headlights and foglamps. Use your wipers and ventilation fan to stop the windscreen misting over, and wind the window down a little – often in fog you'll hear something happening ahead before you see it, but sounds are muffled and do not carry much through closed windows.

It is very dangerous to succumb to temptation and cling to the rear lights of a vehicle in front as a kind of 'security'. If it stops suddenly you've had it.

Winter driving

If you have any qualms about your car's state of health for winter conditions, get it fixed before a tired battery, worn tyre or lazy brake gets you into trouble.

Breaking down in winter is even more miserable than in summer. Walking to a phonebox and waiting for a breakdown truck is not much fun in freezing weather.

Checking the battery

If you know your battery is dodgy, replace it before the really cold weather sets in. If you are determined to soldier on with it a bit longer, be sure you have a set of booster cables (jump leads) handy for an assisted start if the car refuses to get going one chilly morning, or at the very least be sure that your motoring organisation membership gives you cover for starting the car at home, and that it is up to date.

Antifreeze

Make sure, before the cold weather starts, that there is sufficient antifreeze in the cooling system. If there is none, or it is too diluted, you risk the engine freezing up on a frosty night. This could mean the car failing to start the next day, because ice will freeze the water pump rotor and prevent the engine from turning when you use the starter. Ice can also crack the components, presenting you with a large bill for repairing a cracked sump or engine block.

Tyre pressure and tread

The condition of the tyres is especially vital in winter. Those four rubber footprints are a car's only contact with the road surface, and if the treads are worn they will provide too little grip on a damp and cold or icy road.

Ignore anyone who advises you to lower your tyre pressures for better grip on winter roads. Stick to the ones recommended in your car's handbook, or by the tyre manufacturer, as under-inflated tyres wear unevenly, and ultimately grip less well than if they had been maintained at the correct pressures in the first place.

Fuel

Never let the fuel tank slip low during the winter months. An unexpected journey could catch you out if there is little petrol in the car, and in winter many rural petrol filling stations tend to close earlier.

Troubleshooting for winter disasters

Equip the car with a few necessities for getting out of trouble, or at least being comfortable, in a breakdown or stuck in snow.

For the car:
   a set of booster cables
   a towrope
   torch
   shovel
   old doormat
   lock de-icer
   screen de-icer
   scraper
   spare can of petrol
   spare bottle of water-antifreeze mixture
   red warning triangle
   basic toolkit

For you:
   first aid kit
   waterproof coat
   thick socks and wellies

On long journeys in winter:
   a few food provisions
   a flask containing a hot drink or soup
   and a bar of two of chocolate, extra jumpers and a rug

Driving technique

Driving in winter calls for extra awareness, care and attention. An incautious turn on the steering, a ragged gear-change or a hasty stamp on the brakes may not matter much in summer – although any of those is an example of poor driving technique – but in winter they tend to be much more perilous.

Nurse the car along, and read the road ahead for signs of potential problems. Slow down where there are overhanging trees, steep banks, or anything else which could suggest damp or shady conditions which encourage black ice on the road surface. Staying out of trouble is far better than trying to cure the problem once you are already in difficulty.

Skidding

A skid does not just happen, it is always caused, and it is almost always the driver who causes it. It's true that there are cases where some kind of sudden mechanical failure can make a car skid, but such cases are very rare and exceptional.

Avoid the danger of skidding in slippery conditions by treating all the car's controls very gently, as if they were fragile. Pretend the accelerator pedal is made of eggshell, the brakes cut glass, the steering wheel porcelain. Avoid going too fast or accelerating suddenly, harsh braking, steering raggedly, and rough gear changes.

Skidding

How to avoid it:

➡ Accelerate gently and smoothly.

➡ Brake gently and smoothly.

➡ Change gear smoothly, don't 'snatch' the gears.

➡ Steer smoothly and avoid sudden changes in direction.

➡ Keep your speed down in slippery conditions.

➡ 'Read' the road ahead to anticipate trouble.

➡ Watch out for ice under trees and in shaded areas.

➡ Ensure your tyres have ample tread so as to ensure a good grip.

How to cure it:

➡ Take the foot off the accelerator.

➡ Depress the clutch.

➡ Steer towards the direction the car is sliding.

➡ Be ready to steer back the other way as the car slows.

If the car does start to skid, try to avoid the inevitable feeling of panic and the risk of overreacting. Take your foot off the accelerator, keep it away from the brake, de-clutch and try to steer in the direction the car seems to be sliding. By de-clutching, you disengage the engine and avoid the danger of the car's power and momentum running away with you. A modern car is remarkably adept at retrieving a sticky situation under its wheels – probably better than you are.

A good investment for those facing having to drive in icy conditions is a skid control course. These are normally run by commercial organisations, normally at motor racing circuits. Contact your road safety officer to find out about the one nearest you.

Snow driving

Give yourself plenty of time in snow, and do not do anything too quickly. In particular, avoid last-minute, panicky braking; this is a recipe for deep trouble. Because ice or snow is so slippery, it takes much longer to stop the car – two or three times the normal dry road stopping distance. That means thinking ahead and braking much earlier than normal. The danger is that putting the brakes on at the last minute will simply lock up the wheels and start the car sliding across the icy surface, and when that happens, the wheels will no longer react to your steering. To avoid it use 'cadence braking' whenever the surface is slippery: pump the brake pedal up and down rather than stamping solidly on to it. This enables you to pull up more effectively than if the car is sliding, and at the same time you will still be able to steer out of harm's way.

The higher the gear you can stay in without making the engine complain, the better. That enables the engine to run at lower revs for a given speed, and to give the wheels maximum grip without making them spin.

If the road is really icy or you are in thick snow and you cannot even get enough grip to get going in the first place, try driving the car just a fraction backwards and forwards a few times, and then try to pull away in high gear. If that does not work, put a piece of sacking, or a rough mat, under the driving wheels – if you are not sure which they are, there is an easy way to tell: they are the ones that are spinning as you try to make your getaway.

Once on the move in snowy conditions, hills can be a problem. Take a gentle run at a slope, and try to keep the momentum going by moving without stopping at all – best achieved by staying in as high a gear as possible.

Black ice

Black ice is the transparent terror of winter roads. All that really shows of it is an ominous shine on the road surface, but it is a major cause of accidents as cars just slide across it. Whenever the temperature is low, expect black ice and drive accordingly. Take special care in the places where it is most likely to occur – under trees, on exposed hillsides and in the sheltered dips at the bottom of hills – but this does not mean that you might not skate across a patch early one morning on a city road.

Summer driving

Summer is a marvellous time to be on the road. With the roof open and windows down, it is great to pootle along enjoying the scents of summer in open country. But it has its down side, of course, such as holiday traffic jams and hot weather breakdowns. Troublesome insects, hay fever traumas and unexpectedly slippery road surfaces can also catch out the unwary motorist.

Hay fever

If you are one of the millions of unlucky hay fever victims, resist the temptation of driving a convertible car, or one with a large sunroof. It usually helps to drive with the roof and windows closed, relying on the car's ventilation system to filter out at least a little of the incoming pollen. If you can afford it, a car with air conditioning can help tremendously in reducing the miseries of hay fever as air conditioning sucks even less pollen-bearing air. Hay fever sufferers ought to avoid driving if at all possible when the pollen count hits the heights of discomfort, and it is most important not to risk driving if the antihistamines you take make you drowsy. If so, ask your doctor to prescribe an alternative.

Insects

Being suddenly confronted with a large wasp or bee, buzzing around your head at 70 mph on the motorway, can be an extremely unnerving experience. Even a pesky common fly is an irritating distraction.

Insects are prolific in summer, so keep a can of insect spray tucked somewhere handy. Take care to stow the can out of direct sunlight, where it will not get too hot when the car is left parked.

Try and open a window before you start spraying, or else you, too, may be overcome by the noxious fumes with which you aim to exterminate your unwanted passenger. Ideally pull in to the side of the road and deal with the insect while the car is stationary. If you have an objection to insecticides, carry an old newspaper, either to shoo away the brute or to swat it, but in this case also pull over and stop before taking action.

Heat problems

Do not drive too far in hot weather without taking a break, and remember to carry sufficient water or soft drinks. Heat exhaustion is a real danger if you spend hours cooped up in a hot car.

Take care about leaving any cassettes for a car tape-player within range of the sun. They are best stowed in the dark, in the coolest place in the car – under a seat, for example – to avoid being damaged by exposure to excessive direct heat.

Slippery roads

Although we usually think of slippery roads as a problem in autumn or winter, surfaces can be unexpectedly slippery after a shower of rain following a long dry spell. Road surfaces become highly polished if they remain unwashed by rain for a lengthy period in warm weather, as deposits of rubber build up because of the scuffing of tyres as traffic travels fast along them. They can then become quite lethal when suddenly coated with a surface of water.

Such conditions are as slippery and as dangerous as ice, in a way more so. Most of us drive sensibly in winter if we think the roads might be icy, but in summer we assume surfaces are safe and we are not prepared for skidding.

Breakdowns

The motoring organisations dread the first blistering hot days of summer almost as much as the first viciously cold snap of winter. In either case, the number of motorists breaking down and calling for help soars dramatically.

The big summer breakdown hazard is overheating, usually caused by elderly, cracked or perished cooling system hoses which finally give up the ghost in a sweltering traffic jam.

Solid traffic in warm weather catches out lots of poorly maintained cars, not only with leaking hoses, but also dicky thermostats, electrical ailments and other assorted casualties of wear.

Holiday driving

Have the car serviced before embarking on a long holiday run, or at the very least run through your maintenance checklists (see pages 29–31) and make sure the car is mechanically healthy.

One fairly common failure which can catch you out on a warm day is when the car refuses to start after being left standing briefly at the end of a long, fast, hot drive. It is caused by vaporisation of petrol in the fuel line, and is very simply cured. Open the bonnet and let the car cool down for about 20 minutes without making any further attempt to start it. Then it will usually start quite normally.

Luggage

It is very tempting to take a kitchen-sink approach to loading the car for a holiday trip, but it can also be hazardous and at the very least uncomfortable. Trying to cram a gallon of luggage into a pint-sized car makes everyone suffer, producing grumpy, cramped passengers who then make the driver irritable. Survey what you plan to pack with a critical eye, and think of elbow and leg room as more important than extra beach towels and games.

Stow heavy objects as low down as possible, and when loading the boot bear in mind that if you are unlucky, you may need access to the spare wheel during the journey.

Do not load up the rear parcel shelf with a great stock of miscellaneous items, and especially not with heavy things. In any accident they would be thrown around inside the car, and could cause injury.

Roofracks

Roofracks must be completely secure. Load them carefully, with heavier items lowest, and tie everything down tightly. If you use a tarpaulin, take care to see that no edges are flapping loose, and that it is tied down well.

Before embarking on any long journey, load the roofrack and go for a short drive to check that it is secure. After starting the holiday journey, stop after 15 to 20 minutes to re-check the rack.

Never leave an empty roofrack on the car when it is no longer needed. It causes extra wind noise, and the additional drag will not help with cutting down on fuel consumption.

Towing

One solution to the problem of too much luggage and too little space to put it is to stow the overflow into a trailer and tow it behind. However, some of us tow not from overloaded necessity but for pleasure or leisure. I often drive in the summer with the family sailing dinghy hooked on the back, and towing is a regular way of life for caravanning enthusiasts.

How to assess what you can tow

Weight: As a sensible guideline, do not allow the weight of the caravan or trailer, fully laden, to exceed 85 per cent of the kerbside weight of your car (as specified in the handbook).

Power: The suitable level of engine power for satisfactory towing should be at least 40 bhp for each ton of total combined laden (including luggage and passengers) weight of the car and trailer. So, for example, typical combined laden weight of 1.7 tons should have at least a 68 bhp engine pulling it.

Towing has its pitfalls. A bad match between trailer and towing vehicle can be potentially hazardous, and manoeuvring in a confined space with a trailer on the back is tricky for the inexperienced.

Trailer and tow-car must be well matched. It is useless to hook an elephantine trailer onto the back of a Mini and expect the resulting combination to be safe or sensible. The car must be muscular enough for the size and weight of trailer you ask it to pull.

A combined car and trailer are considerably longer, often wider and certainly heavier than a car alone, and so affect the car's behaviour. Steering, braking and acceleration all suffer: the car becomes more sluggish, takes a little longer to stop, and the steering feels heavier than you would usually expect. Your driving, therefore, has to change accordingly.

If towing you also need to plan more time than usual for a journey, to allow for the slower speed at which you will travel and the extra time it takes to exit at junctions or overtake slower vehicles. When driving, you need to leave more space than normal between yourself and other vehicles, to give yourself room for the car's slower responses, and to think ahead, so as to avoid having to brake or change direction suddenly.

Route planning becomes more important than ever before. Plan your journey for the trailer's convenience, avoiding if possible any awkwardly narrow, twisting lanes, U-shaped bends and hump-back bridges.

Time your journey to miss rush-hours, which become even more of a nightmare than normal when you try to negotiate them with a double-length vehicle.

If you want to buy a trailer or caravan, check in the car handbook for the kerb weight of your car. The guideline which the Caravan Club and the National Caravan Council recommend for people who are new to towing is that the fully laden weight of the trailer should never amount to more than 85 per cent of the towing vehicle's kerb weight.

Another useful general guideline is to check the power output, expressed as the brake horsepower or bhp, of the car to be used for towing. This can also be found in the car handbook. Then work out the total weight of everything the engine will have to pull, that is the car's weight plus the weight of the trailer fully laden. Aim for at least 40 bhp of engine power for every ton of combined weight.

The choice of a tow-bar is important, and it must be fitted very securely. It is not worth cutting corners on a cheap one. Choose a reputable brand name, and have it fitted either by a towing specialist or by a dealer franchised for your make of car.

From the legal point of view, you only need a normal full driving licence to qualify you for towing a trailer, and normal car insurance usually covers the trailer too – but not necessarily its contents. Check with your insurance company if in doubt. Remember that a trailer must have a set of rear lights, and it must also display a number plate showing the car's registration number.

Lower speed limits apply when you are towing. The top speed at which you can travel is 50 mph on ordinary roads (providing no lower speed limits apply) and 60 mph on dual carriageways and motorways.

The trickiest thing about towing is reversing. As any articulated lorry driver will tell you, when you reverse with something hooked on behind, everything happens in reverse. You have to turn the steering wheel in the opposite direction to what you would normally expect. In other words, you do not steer to the left to reverse around a left-hand corner, you steer to the right instead.

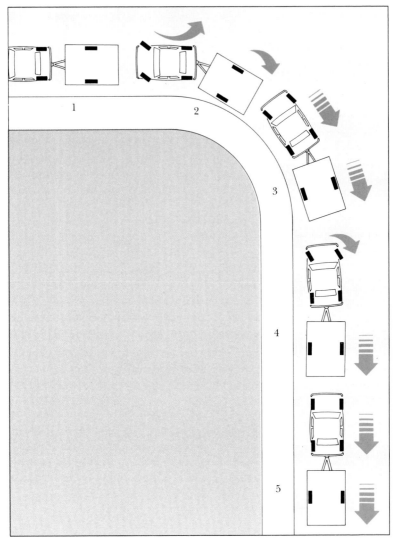

How to reverse a caravan or trailer round a corner. 1, Begin reversing with wheels straight. 2, Steer right to move the trailer left. 3, Steer to the left to ease the trailer's rate of turn. 4, Continue to steer left to straighten the trailer. 5, Continue reversing in a straight line.

The only safe way to get the feel of this is to practise in controlled conditions away from other traffic – an empty supermarket car park on a Sunday morning, for example. If you still can't get the hang of it, contact the Caravan Club, who run courses in towing techniques, or your local road safety officer, who will advise you on any local courses available.

Driving alone

Driving on your own can be an enormous pleasure, but also sometimes a worry. Well-publicised attacks on lone women drivers whose cars have broken down have raised some motorists' feelings of vulnerability – not only women, but many older drivers, and some who are disabled.

These are some ways of looking after your safety if the prospect of being stranded at the roadside alone worries you:

➡ A positive attitude helps. Lone journeys over long distances with just the car radio for company can be very satisfying. Be intent on enjoying the trip.

➡ Prepare well. It is obviously foolhardy to drive late at night, in poor weather, in an ailing car, and expect to have a stress-free journey. Leave nothing to chance: make sure both you, and your car, are in perfect health and well equipped to cope with any emergency which could possibly arise.

➡ Never ignore faults on the car. Don't embark on any long trip, especially one through remote country roads or after dark, unless you are sure the car is in tip-top condition. Keep it regularly serviced and scrupulously maintained.

➡ Route-plan thoroughly. Plan your journey on a good map and familiarise yourself with the route to avoid needless diversions. Getting lost raises the stress factor and puts you in even greater difficulty if you are unlucky enough to break down.

➡ Keep your motoring organisation membership up to date, and be sure to carry the card and relevant phone numbers, and coins or a phonecard, with you.

➡ Keep an emergency kit in the car. A torch, spare can of petrol, rug, flat walking shoes and basic tool kit are essentials .

➡ If you are female, never leave shoes in the car footwell or on the passenger seat. They simply advertise to anyone who happens to glance in that the car belongs to a woman. Always put your handbag on the floor and tucked out of sight, rather than driving with it on a seat and in view.

➡ When driving in town, and always when driving alone at night, keep the car doors locked.

➡ After dark, try to stick to main roads or busy routes wherever possible, as an added protection.

➡ Do not be tempted to pick up hitch-hikers, however innocent they look.

➜ Be aware of other vehicles around you on the road: if you ever think you are being followed, head straight away for a busy area where you know there will be a lot of people about, or drive to the nearest police station.

➜ Plan your parking. Never park in a lonely or concealed spot, and at night choose somewhere well lit. If you are parking in daylight but likely to return to the car after dark, bear in mind how well the location is likely to be illuminated. In multi-storey car parks, look for a space near a ramp or exit.

➜ When returning to your parked car make sure you have the keys ready in your hand, so you won't need to stop and fumble for them.

➜ If you break down and need to call the emergency services, tell the telephonist that you are a woman travelling alone: the police now use a code to alert patrols to give priority to any breakdown calls involving a lone woman, and breakdown services give priority to the 'vulnerable'.

➜ If anyone tries to harrass you on the road, try to drive away from trouble. Stopping to argue puts you at more risk than if you keep going.

Family motoring

Driving with the family can and should be a most pleasurable experience. Most children love cars: a car spells activity, the excitement of going somewhere, the prospect of seeing and doing new things, and the family car is a passport to new experiences shared with those closest to us.

However, it does not always turn out like that. For some families, travelling in the car is more trauma than pleasure; some kids and cars seem to mix like oil and water. In such cases the real problem may well be a lack of adequate planning and preparation. Last-minute panic is not the way to achieve unstressful family car journeys, as children are happiest when things are well organised and orderly.

There are several important factors in successful travelling with children, particularly younger ones. They need to be comfortable, not cramped, be able to see out of the car, have their physical needs adequately catered for, and be kept occupied to avoid boredom.

For the sake of sheer common sense, as well as to satisfy the law, they must also be securely strapped in for their own safety. But they must not be confined for long periods without the chance to get out and stretch their legs. Journeys should be planned with regular stops anyway; with youngsters it is even more essential, to let them unwind. Don't drive for more than three hours without a stop, however much you want to clock up the miles.

Comfort

Always dress for comfort in the car. Loose, comfortable clothing is much the best, especially for a long journey. Bulky sweaters and anoraks are bad news, and so is anything tight-fitting. If a child feels restricted, too hot, or simply too cluttered up with clothing, he or she is liable to travel badly and make everyone else in the car well aware of his or her discomfort.

It is also important to keep the car at the right temperature, which should be as cool as you all feel comfortable with. Turning up the heater and making the car too warm for a long trip makes everyone feel either drowsy, nauseous or grouchy, any of which is bad for any passengers, especially children. It can also be hazardous for the driver, which potentially puts everyone in the car at risk.

On any long car journey it is helpful to have a supply of snacks and drinks readily available. Avoid chocolate, which is both sickly and messy, but boiled sweets or barley-sugar can be useful for keeping up the spirits of older children, and plain sweet biscuits or sponge fingers are safe bets for younger ones. If you prefer to avoid sweet things entirely, keep a supply of apples, bananas and crisps on hand, and have some prepared sandwiches to keep young appetites at bay between meals. Children will often complain of being hungry if they are bored.

Adequate stocks of suitable fluids to quench everyone's thirst are essential, especially in summer. Packeted fruit drinks are convenient, but ideally avoid anything which might stain if it spills, such as blackcurrant.

Older teenagers and adults will appreciate a vacuum flask of tea or coffee, and it gives you the freedom to stop when you are thirsty, rather than waiting for a wayside café to loom on the horizon.

A summer holiday drive is often the longest family car journey of the year. Everyone is excited, and the children especially tend to be full of pent-up energy. A few light exercises, bending and stretching, during a mid-way stop can be a very valuable way of reviving tired limbs and flagging spirits – each year during the height of the holiday season, West Country police encourage drivers to take part in a bit of knee-bending exercise at motorway services on the M5. It is an example worth copying.

Avoiding travel sickness

Car sickness is a very common problem. Some adults are prone to it, but more often it is young children who are affected, and when a youngster is involved it can be particularly distressing and difficult to deal with.

For some unlucky families, going anywhere by car is a road to misery. Everyone waits with bated breath for the seemingly inevitable moment when the wail will go up in the back: 'Mum, I'm going to be sick...', or worse, when it happens without warning.

Curing car sickness is not easy. Anyone who suffers from it persistently should consult a doctor, in case there is some medical cause. But there are a number of ways to avoid car sickness in the first place, and if preventative measures work, there will be no need for a cure.

These are some of the most common triggers for motion sickness: lack of fresh air, cramped or restricted seating and poor car suspension. If scrupulously avoided, the problem may disappear.

Causes of car sickness

➜ *Excessive warmth.* Keep the car at a comfortable temperature, as cool as possible without making the passengers chilly.

➜ *Stale air.* Keep the car well ventilated. Ensure a good flow of air, but avoid direct draughts blowing onto youngsters.

➜ *Too much rich food in the tummy.* Avoid heavy, fatty or over-rich meals immediately before a journey, and allow no sickly sweets on the trip. Sucking barley-sugar or clear mints can help.

➜ *Dehydration.* Avoid it with a ready supply of soft drinks, or preferably still mineral water is the safest option. Persuade them to sip it little and often, rather than waiting until they are fractious and thirsty, and then gulping a cupful at once.

➜ *Sitting too low down.* If a child feels the motion of the car without being able to see where it is going, he or she may well become susceptible to sickness. Ensure the child sits high enough for a good view out of the windows.

➜ *Sitting too long in one position.* Do not stint on regular breaks in a long journey.

➜ *Too energetic a driving style.* Eager acceleration, sudden braking and a 'swirling' style round corners are not conducive to passenger comfort.

➜ *Poor suspension,* such as worn shock absorbers. Where car sickness cannot be resolved by any other means, check out the car for mechanical flaws.

➜ *Reading on the move.* Many people are affected by nausea when looking down in a moving car. Occupy children with 'I-Spy' type games rather than letting them become absorbed in books.

➜ *Boredom and fatigue.* Music can be valuable in soothing irritable, sickness-prone children. Choose something gentle and rhythmic, rather than brash, aggressive pop. Younger children enjoy listening to story tapes, and older ones can be kept occupied with travel tapes talking about the areas through which you are passing.

If all else fails, and someone in the family still suffers persistently from car sickness, then at least prepare well for the worst. Carry a car sickness kit, including some plastic bags, absorbent paper and a freshen-up pack of absorbent wipes, plus an aerosol of a neutral-smelling air freshener. And take heart; most children grow out of it in their early teens.

Games on the move

Children generally have a low boredom threshold, and need to be kept occupied. However excited they may be about the journey, a selection of toys, games and other things which interest them are invaluable on a long drive.

Story tapes to be played in the car cassette player are an excellent way of keeping young minds occupied while still allowing them the freedom to keep their heads up looking out of the window.

Games in which all the family can be involved can make a long drive seem much more pleasant and sociable. I-Spy is the old favourite, but has its complications. Make it a rule that any object outside the car must be one which remains visible for a time, and is not something that is quickly out of sight.

Counting games are useful mile-eaters. Give each member of the family a subject of similar frequency to count, such as cows, sheep and telegraph poles, or churches, bridges and yellow rape fields. The winner is the first one to reach a target number.

Choose places on the map which you will pass through and which none of you have seen before. Then take it in turns to guess what the place will be like, describing buildings and scenery. The winner is the one whose imagination comes closest to the truth.

Choose a place a few miles ahead, and make bets on how long it will take to reach it. With practice, this can become quite a skilful game, and will help children's perception of time and distance.

Select place names from signposts, and take it in turns to make up stories about them, or limericks that include them.

Another game which helps pass the time for youngsters cooped up in the car is the number plate game. Look out for other vehicles with the letter A on their registration plates, then B and so on to work your way through the alphabet. Do the same with numbers, spotting 1, then 2 and so on.

A repertoire of favourite songs can also work wonders in occupying bored children. Either use a sing-along cassette tape, or take it in turns to lead the singing with favourite tunes.

Make up your own family games to pass the time. An amusing game can ease a journey tremendously, make a long one seem shorter, and keep children's minds off the state of their stomachs.

Child safety

Children travelling by car must be strapped in for their own safety. Common sense dictates it, and so does the law. Where safety restraints are fitted, the law says they must be used.

Ideally any child travelling in a car should be in the back seat, furthest away from the most common danger spot in accidents. If a child under 14 travels in the front passenger seat, it is the driver's responsibility to ensure that he or she is suitably strapped in. For children aged one year or older, that can mean either the standard adult seat belt with a booster seat, or the seat belt used in conjunction with some additional form of child safety equipment. For a child aged one year or below, the law states that an appropriate child restraint must be used.

Children sitting in the back seat have had for some time to wear seat belts if they are available, but since July 1991 it has been compulsory for all rear seat passengers, adults as well as children to do so.

Most sensible parents obviously want to ensure that their children are as safe as possible. So for younger children seat belts need to be used with additional safety equipment, such as specially designed child seats or booster cushions.

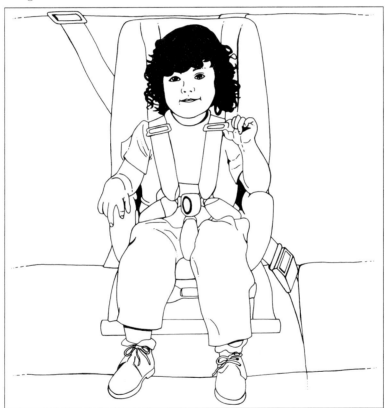

Special child seats are held in place by rear seatbelts.

So long as your car already has rear seatbelts, there is no longer any need to have the car drilled for special straps to keep the children safe in the back. Where rear belts do not exist, and safety harnesses have to be installed, do ensure that they are fitted properly by someone who understands the stresses involved in a collision. Straps must be secured to a strong metal structural part of the car's frame, never to a weak cardboard parcel shelf, for example.

What type of safety equipment should you choose? For tiny babies from birth up to nine months, the safest means of car travel is in a special rearward-facing infant carrier. These are designed to be used in the front seat, with the normal seatbelt looped around through special built-in grooves on the carrier.

From around six to nine months or more, once the baby's neck is strong enough to be capable of supporting the weight of its own head, it can move to the back seat and ride safely in a child seat facing forward.

A booster cushion has integral ears or horns so it can be held in place by a seat belt.

Most of the classic-style child seats are designed for a child from around nine months to between three and four years. Check the label, and let the individual child's body weight, rather than its age, dictate what and when you buy.

Next, from around two and a half to four years, depending on size, a child can move on to a booster seat, which simply raises him or her up so that the adult seatbelt fits more comfortably at a higher shoulder level, held in place by a device on the seat back. From the age of about four just a booster cushion should do.

Don't just use any old household cushion instead, with the intention of saving the cost of a proper booster cushion. If you do, you will put the child at risk of injury in any emergency stop or crash, when an ordinary cushion will catapult forward, with the child possibly 'submarining' out from under the seat belt. A booster cushion is specially designed to stay put in a crash, and is much safer.

Some child safety equipment is available with detachable trays, which provide a playing surface for toys or books. They can be very helpful for keeping the child amused and sweet-tempered on the move.

One important point to bear in mind is that all car safety equipment is designed for once-only use. When it has done its job in a crash, it should then be thrown away and not used again. The forces of an accident can invisibly weaken the structure of a child seat or the webbing of a safety restraint. For this reason, be cautious about using any 'passed down' safety equipment unless you know its history.

All modern cars are fitted with child safety locks on the rear doors. Use them, and check that they are in the safe position every time you go out in the car. It is too late to rue that you forgot to check them when an inquisitive child is leaning across to pull open the door at 70 mph on a motorway.

Pets

I learned from bitter experience how not to transport a reluctant pet in my car when a friend who was moving house asked me if I would drive her two cats to their new home. Soon after we set off the pair fled, tails swishing, to the rear parcel shelf, where they sat and spat at following cars. Then a bicycle swerved out of a side turning ahead of us, and I braked sharply to avoid it.

The cats went beserk, and dashed round the interior of the car, spraying as they went. They survived the journey without further mishap, but the car was never the same again. All the upholstery cleaner and air freshener in the world could not eliminate that distinctive smell.

Cats

Make a cat comfortable in a purpose-made carrier, such as a wicker cat basket with a wire front and a secure clasp. Settle the cat into the basket indoors with a favourite blanket or cushion at the bottom so that it feels at home.

Talk reassuringly to it, and install it the car, either on the front passenger seat where the animal can see you, with the seat-belt looped round to hold the basket in place, or similarly secured on the back seat. It is misplaced kindness to let a passenger cuddle a cat in their arms on the move. Any sudden lurch or change of direction and the result may be a wild-eyed and fleeing cat, badly scratched passenger, and seriously distracted driver!

Small animals, unlike children, do not seem to benefit from being able to see out of the car, but can be unnerved by the confusion of movement around it.

Dogs

Dogs are often easier to handle in the car than cats. Some dogs simply love car travel, and many travel by car regularly on route to a walk or the shops. Big dogs, Labradors for example, often seem content to sit up and look out at the world going by.

However, only let a dog travel freely sitting on a seat if you know from experience that it is docile and familiar with the car. In any case, for safety reasons ensure that the dog travels at the back in the luggage area of a hatchback or estate car, and ideally with a dog-guard metal grating between there and the main passenger compartment. Then, if anything causes it to get agitated or over-excited, it poses no risk to the driver.

Some small dogs are perfectly happy on a rug on the back seat, but it is not ideal. In the event of an accident, a terrified dog could become a very real risk even to its owner, and certainly to any stranger trying to help injured passengers.

There are also specially designed safety harnesses available for dogs. These act like a seat belt to secure the dog into the car and prevent it from being flung forward in an accident, while stopping it from moving about the car.

The best way to transport a dog by car, certainly over any long distance, is in a properly constructed plastic-coated metal mesh carrier, of a suitable size for the dog concerned.

If your dog is particularly nervy, it may need a sedative to calm it down before a long holiday trip. Ask your vet to prescribe one: the dosage depends on the dog's size and weight.

Birds

A cage bird, such as a budgerigar, is best transported in its own cage, but take care to remove any loose or swinging objects which could hurt it in transit.

Cover the cage with an opaque cloth so the bird cannot see out and become confused, and stow it low down in the car – such as in the front passenger footwell or on the floor behind the front seat – so that there is no risk of the cage falling over en route.

Remove any water or seed which may spill, but if the journey is a long one make sure the bird is offered a drink when you stop for a break from the wheel, and talk to it at the same time to reassure it.

If you have cause to carry any farm birds, such as domestic ducks or chickens, use a cardboard box with hay or straw in the bottom. Secure the top tightly, but make sure there are plenty of large air-holes cut into the sides: birds generate a lot of heat in confined spaces.

I have transported hens perfectly happily in this way – and even been rewarded with an egg laid during the journey.

Rodents

Carry rabbits in a stout cardboard box, with plenty of hay or straw at the base, a few holes punched for air circulation, and stowed low down to avoid lurching over.

Other small furry animals, such as hamsters, travel best in their own cages with loose or spillable items removed. It is best to avoid carrying a hamster or mouse in a cardboard box, as you might finish the journey with an empty box, bearing the chewed marks of an escape route.

Fish

Fish can be tricky to transport, by the very nature of the environment in which they live. Water is messy stuff to carry about, but there is a simple and safe way recommended by a vet which I have used, and which poses no particular problems. This is to put the fish in a stout plastic bag half filled with water, leaving a small air space inside when you tie the top. Secure the top of the bag to a metal coat hanger fixed inside the top of a large cardboard box, so that the plastic bag containing the fish is suspended inside it. Stow the box on the floor of the car. Then the fish is safely protected from harm as the car corners, accelerates and brakes.

With all warm-blooded animals and birds, do remember that a stop for a drink during the journey may be necessary, especially in warm weather, and that windows or the sunroof should be left ajar if the car is parked with the animals inside, to let air circulate.

Cold can be just as much a danger as heat if a pet is left too long in a parked car. Pack plenty of warm bedding, or a rug for a cat or dog, and give them a chance to stretch their legs and answer calls of nature as soon as possible at the end of the trip.

Above all, do everything to avoid making the journey uncomfortable for the pet. Not only will the animal suffer but you and your car will inevitably do so too.

Better driving

We all like to think of ourselves as good drivers. Few people are prepared to think there is much wrong with their driving style, even though accident statistics and daily observation of behaviour on the roads suggests otherwise. But in reality there is room for improvement in some aspects of the driving technique of most of us. We should all be ready to admit mistakes, analyse our shortcomings behind the wheel, and attempt to improve our driving standards.

Ask yourself whether any bad habits have crept into your driving, and think about how you could set about amending them. Take a pride in your own driving skill, and work on being a better driver. Arrogance and the assumption that you drive well are things to guard against, and good drivers have the humility to recognise their faults and act on them. Some of the worst drivers are those who think they're terrific.

Defensive driving

Almost any day on any road you can see pushy, impatient drivers who won't give an inch to anyone else. That kind of driving is brainless, tiring, juvenile and, worst of all, hazardous. It is little wonder that more than 90 per cent of road accidents are caused by human error.

However, there is an alternative style of driving which requires intelligence, skill and maturity. It is known as 'defensive' driving, and it is a good style to adopt if only out of the desire for sheer self-preservation.

Defensive driving does not mean crawling about in second gear, but is a method of sensible, responsible car control, as practised by the most experienced and highly trained police drivers. Anyone can learn it. All you need is a strong streak of common sense, a touch of humour, and the intelligence to practise what the experts preach.

The whole key to defensive driving is handling a car in such a way that you always have a safety margin, enough in reserve to enable you to cope with any sudden emergency.

The bible of defensive driving is the police driver's manual, *Roadcraft*, which you can buy in HM Stationery Office bookshops. The system of car control it advocates is summed up in three words, which should be burned deep into the brain of every driver: time to react. They summarise the whole of police teaching on the subject of safe driving, and the essence of handling a car. Plan your driving, think ahead, and do not leave everything until the last moment.

The next time you are driving somewhere and running a bit late, feeling pushed for time, ask yourself honestly whether you are giving yourself enough time to react if another driver does something stupid, if a child runs out into the road in front of you, if a dog dashes off the pavement after a cat, or if a cyclist wobbles into your path out of a side turning.

If the answer is no, then you are a potential accident at risk of finding a location.

A sense of humour is an essential part of defensive driving. It is so easy to let your temper rise when someone stupidly cuts you up on the road, and so tempting to retaliate when a road-hog makes you fume. But a much safer reaction is to simply smile at the other driver's idiocy and dismiss him or her as too stupid to be worth reacting to. Retaliating would only make you an idiot too, however strong the urge.

Defensive driving calls for constant restraint and alertness. It means holding back from rushing headlong into risky situations, and being forever on the lookout for warning signs.

The key to advanced driving

The Institute of Advanced Motorists' chief examiner Ted Clements, a former police class 1 driver, recommends memorising the sentence 'Come and run round this car' as an aid to remembering his six golden rule words:

➡ Concentrate

➡ Anticipate

➡ Relax

➡ Restraint

➡ Think

➡ Courtesy.

*It is a good summary of the basic requirements of defensive driving. You run less risk of having an accident if you always concentrate behind the wheel. You need to **anticipate** the actions of other road users, but it is important to **relax** as you drive to avoid becoming stiff with nervous tension. Exercise **restraint** and hold back when in doubt, and **think** about what you are doing. **Courtesy** to other road users means greater safety for yourself.*

The defensive style of driving is not just a matter of safety, but because it makes you feel more comfortable on the road, it also increases the pleasure of motoring. These are some examples of putting it into action:

➜ Always make sure you have vision and an escape route before overtaking. If there is a bend in the road, a blind brow of a hill, or a side road where another car might turn out in front of you, you must not try to overtake.

➜ Be on the look-out for clues to possible danger ahead. For example, a ball or toy bouncing into the road is an obvious herald of a child potentially close behind it, or a puff of smoke from the exhaust of a parked car can alert you to the possibility of a vehicle pulling out in your path.

➜ Look well ahead, rather than focussing your attention on the car immediately in front. Brake lights suddenly lighting up on a car several vehicles ahead of you can serve as an early warning that the car you are following may suddenly stop.

The canny, defensive driver never glues him- or herself to the tail of the juggernaut in front, blinded by its bulk. It is much safer to sit several car lengths back and just to the left of the crown of the road, so you can see past the truck and a good distance down the road ahead. That way you are ready to overtake when the way is clear to do so safely.

Defensive driving means not being afraid to use your horn when the situation warrants it, such as to let someone know you're there rather than to tell them that you're annoyed with them! If, for example, you are poised to overtake a dawdling driver on a country lane, a quick toot makes sure he is aware that you are there and preparing to pass.

Other aspects of defensive driving involving not forgetting the points made in chapters 6 and 7, especially those relating to leaving a safe gap behind the car in front when driving on a motorway, driving within the range of vision of your headlights at night, and only driving as fast as allows you to see stopping room ahead when it is foggy or raining very heavily.

To some drivers, who are instinctively attracted to a more zippy, cut-and-thrust driving style, this may all sound a bit dull. If so, I hope they are rich (as well as lucky), and can afford the wear-and-tear on their cars. Defensive driving is cheaper. It is less hard on the car, costs less in petrol as it is a more economical style of driving, and it avoids higher insurance costs incurred by lost no-claims bonuses from needless accidents. It is also healthier. Frayed nerves are bad enough for you, let alone crash injuries.

Improving your standards

We can all slip into bad habits, so a constant self-appraisal is essential to maintain and improve your standards of driving. Whether you have been driving for some years, or are newly through the driving test, try to upgrade your knowledge, experience and skill behind the wheel. Seek out specialised books on driving technique, and read as much as you can. Every few years, re-read the book you find most helpful, as a refresher.

One of the best ways of improving your standard of driving is to take additional tuition. Passing the driving test is only the beginning: it legally qualifies you to be in control of a car on the road, but does not make you a good driver. A couple of hours of motorway instruction, for example, can be very beneficial for a newly qualified driver who has never driven on a motorway before, but drivers who passed their test years ago can also benefit from special instruction.

Find out what courses are available in your area. The local road safety officer or the police sometimes run them, so contact the road safety office at the local authority headquarters and ask for details.

If you lack confidence in one particular area of driving, such as parking, driving at night or motorway driving, then it could be worthwhile to invest in some extra lessons with a driving instructor to brush up on the problem zone. Most driving schools, and certainly the British School of Motoring, are perfectly happy to book lessons tailored to a specific need. This does not have to mean going back to school in a car with L plates; the instructor will come with you in your own car.

Bad habits

Ask yourself some searching questions about common bad habits behind the wheel:

➜ Do I persistently exceed speed limits? Driving too fast, especially in the wrong conditions, puts others as well as yourself at risk, and potentially increases the severity of any accident.

➜ Do I accelerate hard and brake sharply? That is an immature, hot-headed style of driving.

➜ Do I not look far enough ahead? Too many drivers concentrate their sights on the back of the car in front. Be much more alert to what is happening as far down the road as you can see.

➜ Do I give insufficient warning of my intentions to other drivers? Last-minute signalling is inconsiderate and dangerous.

➜ Do I ever cut it fine when overtaking or pulling out of side turnings? Beware of familiarity breeding contempt for potential danger. Always leave a good safety margin, or you may not live to regret it.

➜ Do I drive too close to other vehicles? You may think you can stop in time, but failing to make sufficient allowance for the poor reactions of others is asking for trouble.

Advanced tests

If you take a pride in your driving, it can be rewarding to put it to the test and discover whether you have attained the standard of being judged 'advanced'.

What 'advanced driving' means is not rushing about like a racing driver on public roads, but adopting a mature, flowing, considered style which incorporates careful observance of speed limits. It is summed up by the Institute of Advanced Motorists' slogan 'Skill with responsibility'.

Passing an advanced test not only makes you safer and more competent on the road, but can also benefit you financially, since several insurance companies will offer you discounted premiums.

The best known organisation in this field is the Institute of Advanced Motorists. Their test lasts about 90 minutes, and all the examiners are former police drivers who have reached the police class 1 standard, which is recognised as just about the highest level of road driving proficiency in the country.

The test includes town and country driving, with a section on a motorway or dual carriageway, and covers about 35 to 40 miles. That gives the examiner ample time to judge your driving under a wide variety of conditions, and is long enough to ensure that you are driving in your normal manner and not just for a few miles of 'best behaviour'. He is looking for a brisk, purposeful and responsible style of driving, making progress as efficiently as road conditions allow, but without flouting speed limits.

If you are tempted to try the advanced test, but unsure whether your driving would reach the required standards, or nervous of what may be involved, then it could be worth contacting one of the IAM's network of local groups. They have a system which enables potential test candidates to go out for a short drive accompanied by a member who acts as an observer, commenting on whether your driving is of the right calibre and advising on faults which merit improvement.

The other major organisation involved in advanced driver testing is the Royal Society for the Prevention of Accidents. Under RoSPA's scheme, you do not merely pass or fail the test, but are graded according to the level of skill you are judged to have achieved, and can subsequently undergo re-testing to attain a higher grade.

An advanced driving qualification is an achievement and something to be proud of, but not to boast about or to regard as proof of superiority on the road. Like any test, it shows only that you were up to standard on the day in question, and from then on it is important to drive in a way worthy of the badge.

Both testing organisations cherish their reputation jealously, and take a dim view of misdemeanors on the road. Any convictions for motoring offences must be declared, and may cost you your advanced membership.

Useful addresses

➜ Institute of Advanced Motorists: IAM House, 359-365 Chiswick High Road, London W4 4HS, tel. 081-994 4403.

➜ Royal Society for the Prevention of Accidents: Cannon House, The Priory, Queensway, Birmingham B4 6BS, tel. 021-200 2461.

Green motoring

Green is the colour of the 1990s. Caring about the environment, and what we are doing to it, has become an important concern of this last decade of the twentieth century, and it is being reflected in people's attitudes to cars.

It is odd to think that until quite recently green was an unpopular colour for cars. Many people were superstitious about it, and would no more want to drive a green car than walk under a ladder. Because of this, green-coloured cars were traditionally harder to shift on the second-hand market than similar ones in another colour.

Now even green-painted cars are becoming more popular. We motorists, no less than anyone else, have become keenly aware of the environment and what effect we may be having on it.

In my early years as a motoring writer, the most popular question I was asked about a car was, 'What'll it do?', meaning how fast would it go. Top speed and performance were a prime concern and talking point for anyone interested in cars.

That has not entirely changed, but today it is just as common to be asked what a car does to the gallon. The type of fuel we pump into our tanks has changed too. Leaded petrol is gradually disappearing as all new cars can run on cheaper, 'greener' unleaded, and catalytic converters have become a standard feature of newer engines.

Some people might argue that a car is incapable of being kind to the environment, that the fact that it exists at all means that natural resources have been used in its production, it burns precious fossil fuels, and its presence on the road adds to the congestion and noise of urban life. Might we not all give up our cars and walk or cycle instead? Maybe so in a utopian world. But given that cars do exist and give people a flexible mobility few of us would willingly give up, then at least the cars we all drive should be as 'green' as possible.

Exhaust emissions

Until a few years ago, the only real concern most motorists had about what came out of their cars' exhaust pipes was whether belching black smoke told a tale of trouble in the engine.

Now car owners are much better informed about the exhaust emissions and the pollutants they contain. They realise that the combustion process which burns an air-fuel mixture inside the engine to produce the power to run a car inevitably has some undesirable by-products: carbon monoxide, nitrous oxide and hydrocarbons. However, the quantities vary according to the efficiency of the engine and how well tuned it is, which is one important reason why maintaining a car in a good state of tune is so important, and why that is now included in the MOT test.

In older cars that still can only be run on leaded petrol, there is another unpleasant toxin in the exhaust fumes: lead. Concentrations of it in the atmosphere are a danger to health, particularly to the brains of young, growing children.

Around the world, stricter legislation is forcing motor manufacturers to clean up exhaust emissions and meet tougher standards on permitted levels of pollutants. Japan and southern California have been at the forefront in forcing the pace towards tighter controls, because of the particular problems caused by their geographical features. The word 'smog' might have been invented with Tokyo or Los Angeles in mind. But the sheer numbers of cars have led to tougher regulations throughout much of the rest of the world as well, Europe and Britain included. In particular, EC regulations have effectively set a deadline of 1 January 1993 by when all new cars sold in Britain and the rest of the European Community have to be fitted with standard catalytic converters, to detoxify the pollution coming out of their exhaust pipes.

The fuel in your tank

Petrol

Petrol consumption started to become an issue in the early 1970s, when the first major fuel crisis focussed attention on the quantity of the world's natural resources our cars consume. Then during the 1980s another fact of a car's fuel consumption started to dawn on people. All the same, it took years of campaigning by CLEAR, the Campaign for Lead-Free Air, to persuade the population at large, and the government in particular, that lead ought to be taken out of petrol.

Why was it added in the first place? The practice dates from the1930s, when lead was found to give petrol a boost which enabled the more powerful car engines that were appearing at the time to run as efficiently as possible.

Now most cars built in the past ten years can run perfectly well without any lead in their fuel, although some need minor retuning. But to understand why some older cars cannot be easily coverted to using unleaded petrol, you have to know about one of lead's incidental properties, namely that it lubricates and protects softer metal parts of the engine. The soft metal in the valve seats of these cars would become pock-marked and damaged if not regularly flushed with lead, resulting in a prematurely aged engine, in need of expensive repairs.

Nevertheless, not all older cars need lead constantly. For some, all that is needed to keep the engine healthy is a tiny amount of lead flushed periodically over the tops of the valves. Therefore, the makers' recommendations for some models are that they should be fuelled with leaded petrol every third or fourth top-up, but can use unleaded the rest of the time.

Modern engines have hardened metal valve seats which are unaffected by the lack of lead washing past them. Hence, for most recent and all new cars, the only modification needed to enable them to use unleaded petrol is one of tuning, to adjust the engine's running to cope with a marginally lower octane.

Because it is not a simple issue, it is vital that any car owner sticks strictly to the manufacturer's advice on use of unleaded petrol. Do not take a chance on topping up with much cheaper unleaded petrol unless you know for sure that it suits your car.

In time, all the older cars which cannot use unleaded will reach the scrapyard, and the vast majority of cars on the road will use clean petrol with no lead added. Future generations will grow up more healthily without the risk of impairing intelligence through breathing contaminated air.

Diesel

Traditionally a heavy vehicle fuel, diesel has become increasingly popular for cars in the past few years. Sales of diesel cars in this country have increased twenty-fold over the past decade, and although still a relatively low proportion at around one in ten total new car sales, they are growing steadily.

The advantages and disadvantages of diesel

Pros

- high fuel economy, especially in urban driving
- longer engine life
- reliability, no ignition system to go wrong
- cleaner exhaust emissions

Cons

- engine tends to be noisier
- not as smooth running as petrol engine
- performance more sluggish
- sooty exhaust if maintenance poor
- fuel smellier, messier

Despite its dirty, smelly reputation, and the connotations with smoke-belching lorries, diesel is in fact a relatively clean fuel. The quantity of toxins in its exhaust emissions is measurably lower than that in a petrol car's exhaust. But diesel's Achilles' heel is sooty particles emitted in the exhaust fumes, which are visible as black smoke coming out of the tailpipes of older vehicles. That can to some extent be overcome by use of filtering devices.

Some of the newer car diesel engines are equipped with catalytic converters to clean their exhaust emissions even further. That trend is likely to grow, and those cars are arguably the cleanest, 'greenest' models on the market.

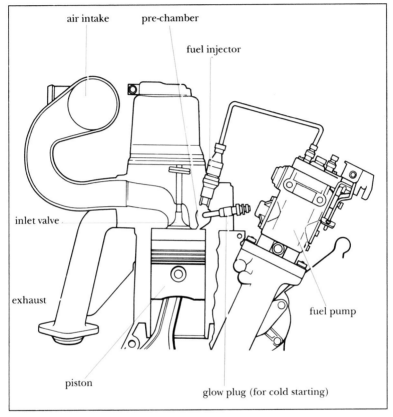

Fuel flow and piston of diesel engine viewed from side.

As well as being less polluting, a diesel engine is between 20 and 25 per cent more economical than a comparable petrol engine. The design of a diesel engine means that it tends to last much longer and to be more reliable than its petrol equivalent. A diesel is slower revving and has no ignition system or spark plugs, because diesel spontaneously ignites at a much lower temperature than petrol and does not need a spark to trigger it.

There is, though, a downside. Diesels are more sluggish than petrol cars with a comparable engine capacity, although many newer diesels are turbocharged to compensate. They are also inherently noisier and tend to vibrate more, disadvantages which manufacturers overcome with extensive use of soundproofing materials.

Catalytic converters

This is the age of the 'cat' – not the feline kind, of course. To be a truly green motorist you should drive a car equipped with a catalytic converter, a device attached to the exhaust system which filters harmful toxins out of the engine's exhaust gases and converts them into something cleaner and safer to breathe.

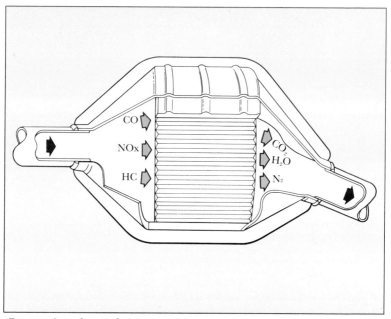

Cross section of a catalytic converter.

The toxic substances which otherwise come out of a car's exhaust pipe – carbon monoxide, nitrous oxide and hydrocarbons – contribute to the formation of photo-chemical smog which hangs over congested city centres in warm sunny weather, and makes city air unpleasant to breathe.

A catalytic converter, or 'cat', is a stainless steel box containing a ceramic honeycomb coated with three precious metals – platinum, rhodium and palladium – which act as catalysts on the exhaust gases coming out from the engine. These gases, which are the toxic waste by-products from engine combustion, pass through the 'cat' and are converted into relatively harmless carbon dioxide, water vapour and nitrogen.

A catalytic converter works like a lung. Although it is relatively compact, usually about a foot long, it has a huge internal surface area. Spread out, the surface of the honeycomb would cover a football pitch.

Cars fitted with catalytic converters must be run exclusively on unleaded petrol, because even minute traces of lead can damage the precious metal coating inside the 'cat'.

Unfortunately, you cannot simply add a catalyst to an existing car and instantly clean up its exhaust. First, the car needs a stainless steel exhaust system to last the life of the vehicle, so that once installed the catalyst never has to be moved. Next, it must have fuel injection and an engine management system, to ensure that the flow of petrol through the engine and of gases into the catalytic converter is strictly regulated. Another complication is that you have to find space to fit the catalyst at the top of the exhaust system and as close to the engine as possible, because it has to heat up quickly to do its job properly. Cars not designed in the first place to have a 'cat' do not necessarily have room under the bonnet for one.

All of that explains why it is not cheap to install a catalytic converter, highly desirable though it may be for the environment, in a car which did not originally come equipped with one. The price can run to many hundreds, and in some cases thousands, of pounds.

Driving for economy

How to improve your mpg

If you want to improve your mpg, follow these guidelines:

➜ Avoid flooring the throttle. It slurps fuel. Accelerate gently and progressively to build up speed.

➜ Avoid hard braking. It scrubs off the momentum which has taken precious fuel to build up.

➜ Where there is obviously going to be a hold-up ahead, back off the power early so that only light braking is needed to slow the car.

➜ Try to pace your driving to catch traffic lights as they turn green, rather than rushing up and having to wait while they are still red.

➜ If you get stuck in a traffic jam and obviously face a delay, switch off the engine to avoid wasting fuel.

➜ Higher gears are more frugal, so use first gear only to pull away and change up through the gearbox as quickly as possible.

➜ Stay in as high a gear as suits the prevailing conditions, and when there is no particular need to hurry, choose a cruising speed which feels relaxing rather than rushed. Many cars are at their most economical at around 50 mph in top gear.

➜ In hilly country, when there is not too much other traffic about, build up speed on downhill stretches to give you momentum for uphill gradients without having to put your foot hard down on the throttle.

➜ Pace your driving to take advantage of overtaking gaps with a smooth, flowing and progressive style, rather than having to brake behind another vehicle and then accelerate past it.

There are many aspects to greener motoring, not all determined by the manufacturers. Using less fuel, for example, is a useful conservation measure, as well as helping to save money on running costs.

If you want to drive more economically, the first question to ask yourself is: "How heavy is my right foot?" Even if you do not know the answer, your car undoubtedly does. The more weight it feels stomping on its accelerator and brake pedals, the thirstier it will be for fuel.

Uneconomical driving is so wasteful that you might just as toss coins out of the car window at regular intervals. Rushing up to traffic lights and then slamming on the brakes, tearing about in low gear, and driving about with an empty roofrack on top of the car or a boot full of unnecessary objects are all the habits of a spendthrift. So is driving with the tyre pressure too low.

It is a pity that so many drivers seem to treat their cars that way, because economy-minded motoring not only saves fuel, it also reduces the wear and tear on the car, and is less stressful on the most vital component of all – the one holding the steering wheel. But however careful you are about driving economically, never do so at the expense of safety.

When you next change your car, put fuel economy high on the list of priorities for the new one. Who needs a slurping big car when a less thirsty smaller one will do just as well? That is especially true if most of the car's life is spent driving to the shops or to the station, taking the kids to school, commuting to the office, and other local journeys with only an occasional trip up the motorway thrown in.

The current generation of small hatchbacks are remarkably versatile, practical and comfortable. Bigger cars may boast higher top speeds, but as the legal limit is 70 mph in this country and not much more than 80 mph across most of the continent, high performance tends to be academic.

Unless you drive constantly in town, a manual is preferable to an automatic because it is more economical.

Switching to a diesel is worth considering if you really want to improve your fuel economy, and especially if the car is used mostly for urban journeys.

When not to drive

Perhaps the most environmentally friendly car of all is the one you leave at home when the journey is short enough for an alternative method of travel, such as walking.

In our mobile age, it is very tempting to use the car at every opportunity, even for a very short trip to the shops, or to visit a friend who lives nearby. Cars are so convenient, so easy, that we rarely stop to think whether a trip is really necessary.

Lots of stop-start journeys are not good for a car. In such conditions it is running cold, with no time for its engine to warm up and reach its most efficient temperature. As a result it uses proportionately more fuel than on longer journeys, and burns it less efficiently, which is bad for the environment. It is not good for you, either.

Just as television turns some slothful viewers into 'couch potatoes', so excessive reliance on the car can turn some lazy motorists into 'driving seat potatoes'. To avoid being one, use your legs rather than your wheels for very short trips.

Dealing with emergencies

Sooner or later every driver faces some kind of emergency outside normal experience. The first time any particular disaster occurs it can be daunting and unnerving, but already knowing the correct procedures for coping can go a long way to making it less traumatic. Take care, then, to prepare in advance by memorising what to do, rather than referring to advice when it is too late.

Much of the sting of potential problems can be defused by taking out motoring organisation breakdown cover, so that you can summon help when an emergency arises.

Breakdowns

When the car grinds to a halt with a breakdown, it is generally more of an inconvenience than a dire emergency. But a car stranded in an awkward situation is a different matter if it endangers other traffic, and if it is causing an obstruction, you must try to move it if at all possible. If for some reason that is impossible, then at least ensure that other drivers are made aware of its presence. Ideally, always carry a red warning triangle for this purpose. Under international law it should be positioned 100 metres behind the stationary car on motorways, and 30 metres behind the car on all other roads.

It seems to be one of the more irritating aspects of car ownership that when a breakdown happens, it is least likely to be on a mild, sunny day when you are out for a leisurely spin. Far more

---

What to do when you break down

➜ If possible move the car away from danger well off the road.

➜ Ensure the handbrake is on.

➜ Take a careful note of your location, including road name and number, any nearby junctions or landmarks.

➜ Be sure you know the registration number, make, model and colour of your car.

➜ Secure the car with doors locked and valuables in the boot before leaving it to summon help.

➜ Exit by a door away from the traffic, especially if on a motorway.

➜ Take your AA, RAC or other breakdown service card with you when going to phone for assistance.

likely is when you are in a hurry to get somewhere important, at night on a dark country lane, when it is raining , or all three at once.

Always keep the car prepared for the possibility of breakdown, because they happen so easily and unexpectedly to cars new and old. If the car is covered by a breakdown service under warranty, or if you are a member of a motoring organisation with breakdown cover, be sure to have the card with you and the relevant telephone number accessible. Keep a stock of suitable coins and phone cards in the glovebox – and make sure you do not raid this money to put in parking meters and then forget to replace it.

Ensure that there is always a map in the car, so that if you do break down you can clearly describe where you are, including the relevant road number. Misunderstandings over where the car is are a common reason for breakdown services taking a long time to reach it.

If you have to leave the car to go and summon help, ensure that it is left locked, with the hazard warning lights on, and with any valuables stowed out of sight. Otherwise a breakdown could cost you more than just lost time.

Electrical faults
Electrical faults are among the most common causes of breakdown. They can be caused by component failure, but more often stem from damp in the car's electrical system. If the car refuses to start after being parked for a time in damp weather, or grinds to a halt in a rainstorm, it is quite likely to be due to moisture in a crucial place.

You can often avoid the need to call for professional help simply by keeping an aerosol can of moisture-repellant spray in the car. Spray it as directed on the can: around the distributor cap, plug leads and electrical cables.

If a piece of electrical equipment which is not essential to the car's safe running is playing up, use the handbook to identify which fuse controls it, and as a temporary measure remove that particular fuse to disconnect the problem item.

Fuel starvation
Fuel problems are also high up the causes of breakdowns. Sometimes a fault develops in the fuel feed system, such as a blockage in the carburettor, which has to be cleared, but only tackle such a fault yourself if you are sure you know what you are doing. Petrol is flammable, and hence a serious hazard for an inexperienced amateur trying to effect a repair.

Much more often, however, shortage of fuel is simply a matter of the tank running dry. Car fuel gauges are notoriously untrustworthy, so do not take chances by running the fuel too low. Running out of petrol is not just a nuisance but makes you look pretty silly too.

Overheating

The third common cause of breakdown is overheating. You are usually warned when it is about to happen by an ominous steamy smell starting to permeate the inside of the car. Do not ever ignore this and hope it will go away. Stop and check the cause, and you will probably find steam rising from the radiator.

If that is the case, do not attempt to do anything about it for a good 10 to 15 minutes, otherwise you risk being badly scalded by a rush of boiling water as you release the pressurised radiator cap.

Once the engine has had time to cool down a little, wrap something protective around your hand, grasp the radiator cap, and – leaning backwards to keep your face well clear of a sudden gush of scalding steam – gently undo it. If it starts to whoosh, let that subside before taking the cap right off.

Do not be tempted to top up immediately with cold water while the radiator is still very hot. If you can obtain some warm water for topping up, use that. If not, let the car cool down for another 20 to 30 minutes before topping the radiator with cold water.

Overheating should always be taken seriously. It can be caused by something as simple to put right as the coolant level having been allowed to drop too low in hot weather, or it could involve a minor repair such as replacing a split water hose.

It can also result from a faulty thermostat or electric fan failure. If the car overheats, and does so again despite ensuring that the coolant is fully topped up, then you must establish the cause before driving any further. You risk engine damage if you try and drive on with the car running perilously hot.

A common cause is a broken fan belt and it is wise to carry a spare in case. You will know if the fan belt breaks because the engine temperature will start to rise and the ignition warning light may come on. In an emergency, a pair of tights twisted to make them shorter and firmer, and tied securely in place, can be used as a temporary fan belt.

Some older cars are prone to running too hot when crawling in a traffic jam in hot weather. If you know your car is liable to overheat, take the precaution of carrying a spare canister of water with you.

Vaporisation

Occasionally, a car may break down in hot weather due to petrol vaporising in the fuel line before it reaches the engine. Having behaved impeccably on a long, fast drive, the car may simply refuse to start again after a brief stop.

This can be cured quite simply by applying something cold to the fuel pump, such as a cloth which has been wrung out in cold water. Usually the problem rights itself if you simply leave the car to stand to cool down for a while, at least 15–30 minutes, with the bonnet open.

Tyre and wheel problems

As the car's only contact with the road, tyres are crucial to its safe progress, and any problem involving them should be dealt with promptly and carefully.

Happily, punctures are rare occurrences. Statistics from the tyre industry suggest that a puncture happens on average for the typical motorist only about once every five years. Modern car tyres are built not only to last a long time, but to stand up to a lot of punishment.

The bad news is that when a puncture happens, it is almost bound to be at a very inconvenient moment. Every motorist should therefore be capable of changing a wheel. Lack of strength is not a good enough reason for being stranded by a puncture, as insufficient muscle power can almost always be overcome by knowing the right technique.

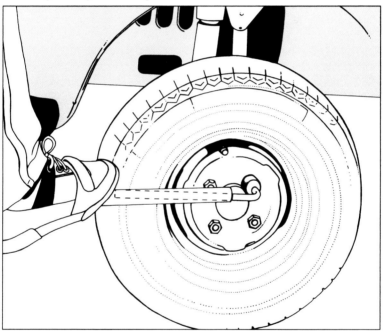

Removing tight wheel nuts.

Women commonly complain of being unable to undo over-tightened wheel nuts. What you need in this case is something to provide extra leverage, and your own weight will do the trick. Position the wheel-brace so that the jutting-out bit is horizontal, and then stand on it – put one foot on the end of the brace, grip the car body with your hands, then lift your other foot up off the ground so your whole weight is being used to shift the nut. Alternatively, wedge the car jack on the end of the brace to create a longer arm on which to exert a bit of extra force, by increasing the amount of leverage. I have yet to find a stubborn wheel nut

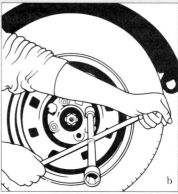
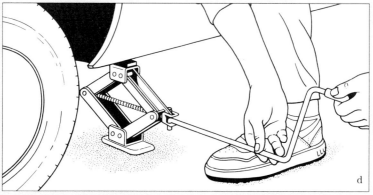

Changing a wheel

1   Ensure that the car is on reasonably level ground before attempting to change a wheel, and check that the handbrake is on.

2   Prise off the wheel trim and upend it on the ground, ready to be used to stow the wheel nuts, so that there is no danger of their becoming lost or rolling into a drain (**a**).

3   Slacken the wheel nuts in a diagonal sequence, before you jack up the car (**b**).

4   Raise the appropriate corner of the car using the jack at the recommended jacking point (**c**): check the car handbook if you are unsure where this is. Be sure to jack the car high enough for the fully inflated spare tyre to fit onto the hub (**d**).

5   Next remove the wheel nuts and stow them in the upended wheel trim (**e**).

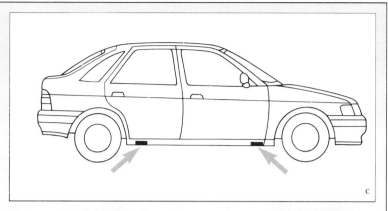

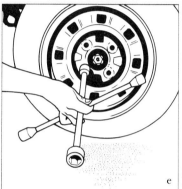

6   Take off the wheel and place on its side under the edge of the car near the jack, as a protection just in case the car slips off the jack for any reason (**f**).

7   Take the spare wheel and position it on the hub. Replace the wheel nuts and tighten them until they are finger-tight.

8   Give the nuts a couple of turns with the wheel brace, then carefully lower the jack.

9   Tighten the wheel nuts as firmly as you can, not in a clockwise sequence, but do one first, then the opposite one, then another and its opposite, and so on.

10 Replace the wheel trim, stow the jack, and take the punctured tyre to be repaired or replaced.

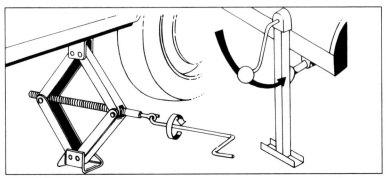

The most common types of jack: scissor jack (left) and a side-lift jack.

which I cannot shift by one of those methods. But if you doubt these methods, buy yourself a telescopic wheel brace and keep it permanently in the boot; it will also give you extra leverage.

Just supposing disaster happens, and while you are changing the wheel, all or most of the nuts go missing. Are you now stranded? Not necessarily. Remove one wheel nut from each of the three other wheels, and use them to secure the fourth wheel. Then drive carefully and slowly to the nearest garage to obtain replacements.

Aquaplaning

The frightening and dangerous phenomenon known as aquaplaning is caused when the front tyres literally start to skate on a surface cushion of water, momentarily out of contact with the road surface.

From the driving seat, the first sign that it is happening is when the steering suddenly goes light, and ceases to respond to the steering wheel, but if you could see the wheels from outside the car, they would appear to be stationary.

The cure is to come right off the power and prepare to steer as soon as the tyres grip again. There are two root causes of aquaplaning: worn tyres which have too little tread to clear away a build-up of water beneath them, and excessive speed for the conditions. To avoid it always slow down on very wet roads.

Blow-out

Every motorist fears a tyre suddenly and spontaneously deflating when travelling at speed, especially on a motorway. When that happens there is a loud bang, and then there may be a strong pull to one side on the steering if a front tyre has blown, or a feeling of the tail end sliding sideways if it is a rear one.

In either case, stay as calm as possible and steer to counter the sideways movement of the car. Steer as smoothly as you can and do not jerk at the wheel or it may worsen the problem. At the same time, back right off the power. If you can manage to do so, hit the hazard warning switch to let other drivers know you are in trouble.

Once the car is back in a straight line and starting to slow down, begin braking progressively to bring the car to a halt.

Try to stop the car on a hard surface, because you will need to change the wheel with the blown tyre, and that will be harder to do if you have stopped on a soft verge.

Loose wheel

If you suddenly hear a clanking sound and find the steering starting to feel peculiar, it could be the warning that a wheel is working loose. Slow down immediately but gently and progressively, and stop to check all the wheels.

If there are loose wheel nuts, tighten them, and then drive to a garage to have all the wheels professionally checked.

The most likely cause of a wheel working loose is the nuts not having been tightened sufficiently the last time the wheel was changed. If you failed to notice the symptoms, the wheel could come off suddenly and the car would drop down at that corner. In such circumstances, the car veers to one side, and you should steer firmly and brake carefully to bring it safely to a halt.

Steering faults

Total steering failure is very rare, and there is almost always some warning that it is about to happen, such as a feeling that the steering seems to wander, or that it seems woolly as you try to turn the wheel. Never ignore symptoms of that kind, but stop the car and investigate what is going wrong.

In an older car with badly worn steering joints, it is just possible that a sudden jolt could make them come apart, and cause the steering to fail. If you are ever unlucky enough for that to happen to you, try to brake progressively to stop the car.

In a car with power steering, it is possible for the power assistance to fail, suddenly rendering the steering very heavy and unwieldy. As you slow down the steering will feel heavier still, so try to brake and pull up where the road is straight if at all possible.

Brake failure

Modern cars have dual braking circuits precisely to ensure that a sudden fault will not leave the car without brakes, thereby making total failure very rare. If one of the circuits does fail, the other one will continue to do its job, although its ability to slow the car on its own will inevitably make the brakes feel less effective than normal.

The most likely cause of a failure in the braking system is a fracture in the hydraulic pressure line. Unless it is a four-wheel-drive vehicle specifically designed for off-road use, avoid subjecting the car to very rough surfaces as the jolting can create this kind of fracture.

If you do ever suffer brake failure, change down quickly through the gears and use the handbrake gently to reduce speed. Do not rush through the gears too fast, or grab the handbrake too hard, or you risk destablising the car.

If you are travelling quickly when you realise the brakes have failed, and have no chance of using gears and handbrake to slow the car in time, your only option may be to deliberately brush the car against a bank or wall at the side of the road to impede its momentum. Better a badly scraped car than a head-on crash.

Brakes can become temporarily ineffective when they get very wet. If you have driven through a ford or flood, dry the brakes by gently applying them a few times as you drive carefully along, until you feel them 'biting' normally again.

Another reason for brakes losing their effectiveness can be when they overheat through excessive use when descending a long hill in top gear, which can cause the brake fluid to vaporise. Cure the problem by slowing down and pumping the pedal rapidly up and down, until the braking system's response to the pedal improves.

Never ignore braking faults or loss of efficiency. If the brakes' performance seem to be deteriorating, have them checked before a mere nuisance becomes a major emergency.

Broken windscreen

Windscreen damage is common, especially in summer as it is the favourite time for road resurfacing. When you see a newly surfaced and freshly gritted road ahead, slow down and keep well clear of other vehicles, to avoid stones being flung up and hitting your screen.

Toughened screens

Older cars have toughened windscreens made of heat-treated, strengthened glass. When struck sharply, such as when hit by a stone flung up from under the wheels of the car in front, they craze into thousands of tiny pieces right across their surface.

If your car has such a screen carry a roll-up emergency windscreen in the boot for temporary use, and keep the telephone number of an emergency windscreen service handy. Driving a car with a toughened windscreen, you may well need it at some point.

If it shatters:

➜ Try to remember what was on the road ahead of you and pull up in a straight line, knocking on your hazard warning lights if you can to warn traffic behind of the sudden emergency. When a toughened glass screen shatters, there is no option but to stop. Try to drive on with it in that condition, and the glass will simply collapse. In any case it is illegal to drive behind an obscured screen.

➜ The sudden bang of a screen shattering will be a shock, but try not to duck or flinch. Do not be tempted to punch your fist through the screen. You'll only end up with a lap full of glass and cut knuckles – or worse. Leave it alone and pull in carefully, using your mirrors and signalling what you are doing.

➔ Use a blanket or newspaper to cover and protect the top of the dashboard and the bonnet, and try to remove the glass carefully outwards, on to another rug or newspaper protecting the bonnet.

➔ If you cannot find a waste bin nearby to dispose of the broken glass, put it neatly in a pile in the gutter, where other cars are least likely to run over it.

When having a new screen fitted, insist on a laminated one as the replacement. It may be dearer, but it has many advantages.

Laminated screen

All the more recent cars have this safer design of windscreen, made of a glass and plastic interlayered sandwich, so that if struck the screen only cracks rather than shattering. Typically it goes in a star or spider's web pattern, stretching outward from the point of impact. Unless the impact which damaged the screen was very severe, you should have no trouble seeing through the glass to drive to a garage for help.

Laminated windscreens are safer and more convenient than the toughened type, and are now the standard fitment on every new car sold. Unlike a toughened screen, a laminated one does not fall apart when it is damaged.

Accidents

If you become involved in a car accident, it will always seem like an emergency, even if the damage is slight. Being involved in a car crash, even a minor one, can put you in a state of shock, but panicking will only make things much worse. Try to stay as calm as possible, and get to grips with the situation.

You should always carry a notebook and pen, and ideally a small camera as well, stowed in the glovebox. Use them to record the scene of the accident, relative positions of the vehicles involved, directions in which they were travelling, weather and road conditions, and the names and addresses of all other drivers and any witnesses.

Some insurance companies supply accident report forms for collecting details at the scene of a crash. If yours does, keep the form handy in the car, ready for when you may need it. Be sure to take the registration numbers and note the makes and models all other vehicles involved. Ask other drivers for details of their insurance cover, even though they are not necessarily obliged to supply them.

Even if you feel responsible for causing a crash in which you have been involved, do not admit blame or rush to apologise, as with hindsight you may regret something said in a state of shock. Both insurance companies and the police advise against admitting liability at the scene of an accident. Exchange details with the other drivers, and leave it to the insurance companies to sort out.

Damage only

If nobody is injured and damage to the vehicles involved in the accident is slight, it is not essential to call the police. However, if the other driver is reluctant to supply a name and address, or appears to have been drinking, it could certainly be wise to do so.

As soon as the accident has happened, check the time. People are often vague later on about details such as the precise time an accident happened and the exact location.

If names and addresses are not exchanged at the scene, take the precaution of reporting the accident to the police within 24 hours, or you risk being accused of failing to report an accident if the other driver complains to the police.

Accidents involving injury

First and most important, when anyone is hurt, is to ensure that they are not in imminent danger. Check that the injured person can breathe and does not have a blocked air passage, that any serious flow of blood is stopped, and that they are not at risk of further injury from other traffic arriving on the scene.

Make sure someone calls for an ambulance and for the police. An ambulance is obviously the first priority, and by law the police must always be notified when a road accident involves injury to someone.

If there is a considerable mess on the road, including perhaps spilled fuel, the Fire Service may be needed to clear and hose down the road surface, and it could save time to call them straight away as well.

While waiting for the emergency services to arrive, stabilise anyone who has been injured. As well as ensuring that they are safe from further harm, keep them warm, reassure them and try not to move them. Do not let too many people crowd in on the injured person. As soon as an ambulance or someone medically qualified arrives, move out of the way to let them take over.

The police will ask you to make a statement. Keep it brief, stick to plain facts and do not admit anything. While you are in a state of shock it is advisable to say as little as possible, especially if you feel you may have been at least partly at fault. Statements taken at the scene of an accident are available to be used as evidence in any subsequent prosecution, and you should be careful to avoid incriminating yourself. When someone is injured, there may also be resulting claims for damages, in which copies of statements could be used in evidence.

Avoid getting involved in correspondence with other drivers after an accident. If you receive letters from other people involved, pass them on to your insurance company.

Animals

If you are involved in a collision with an animal, the law requires you to report it to the police only if it is a dog, horse, sheep, pig, cow or bull, mule or donkey, and if the creature is killed or seriously injured.

You must also, if asked, supply your name and address to anyone who has reasonable cause to want it, such as the farmer who owns the animal.

First aid

Ideally, every car would carry a first aid kit. In some other European countries it is a legal requirement to keep one in the car; here it is not mandatory, but it is good sense to have one. Even a very minor emergency such as an insect sting or cut finger may need attention, and the car should be equipped to cope.

As well as carrying a first aid kit in the car you should have at least a basic knowledge of how to use it in an emergency situation. If not, gen up on a good book from the local library, or enroll in a first-aid course.

Shock

Road accident victims are inevitably in a state of shock, so the prime purpose of first aid is to stabilise the victim's condition, keep him or her calm, warm and as comfortable as possible under the circumstances.

Loosen clothing around the neck and waist, particularly anything tight-fitting. Cushion the head and cover the person with a rug, coat or anything available to keep them warm and reduce the shivering which accompanies shock.

If the person is conscious and in pain, it is best not to move them until help arrives, in case of compounding any injury. If the person is unconscious, carefully move them into the 'recovery' position, lying front down, head to one side, arms forward with elbows bent, and one leg drawn up.

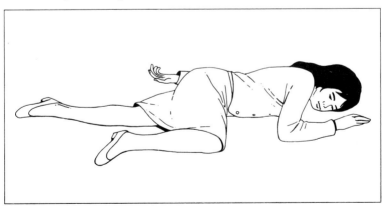

The recovery position.

Breathing

It is essential to ensure that an injured person has a clear air passage and is able to breathe, so make sure their tongue is not blocking the air passage. If the person is not breathing, check that nothing else is blocking the mouth, and then try mouth-to-mouth resuscitation if you know how to do it. If you do not know how, find out as soon as you can and practise it before finding yourself in a situation where your swift help may be a crash victim's only hope.

Loss of blood

The other most serious danger to someone injured on the road is severe blood loss due to blood pouring unchecked from a wound. If you are first on the scene and someone is potentially bleeding to death, forget any squeamishness you may have. Grab anything suitable to make a pad with which you can apply pressure to the wound, and hold it firmly where the blood is coming out. Use more pads and more pressure as necessary to stem the blood flow until help arrives.

Fire

Car fires are frightening. With flammable fuel on board, and a car constructed of materials which burn readily, fire can spread quickly through the passenger compartment.

The best protection for yourself and your car is to carry a good quality fire extinguisher, and keep it readily accessible for use in a hurry. Stowing it in the boot under all the holiday luggage is not the best place.

Action on suspecting an engine fire

➔ First switch off the engine. If a fuel line has fractured, you do not want the engine running and continuing to pump fuel into the fire.

➔ Do not snatch open the bonnet to see where the trouble is. That will only fuel the fire with oxygen and could make it flare up, and you may burn your hand on an already-hot bonnet.

➔ Instead, carefully open the edge of the bonnet just a crack, to see if you can spot where the smouldering is located. Then squirt the fire extinguisher liberally through the crack in the appropriate direction.

➔ Slowly lift the bonnet and be prepared to continue using the extinguisher. Douse the flames liberally, and be prepared to prevent them from re-igniting.

➔ Call the Fire Service, even if you manage to put the blaze out yourself. It could be in danger of it re-igniting for some time afterwards.

Driving abroad

The quirky fact that Britain drives on the left-hand side of the road, while everyone else in Europe drives on the right, makes the experience of motoring abroad all the more interesting, though of course also potentially more hazardous.

Our national motoring eccentricity originates historically in the convenience of armies on the move, which would march on the side of the road where they could have weapons at the ready in their right hands, prepared to confront on-coming foes.

Now we are permanently out of step with the rest of Europe in our driving habits, which can cause complications for anyone planning to drive abroad for the first time. Switching temporarily to driving on the right is not, in fact, difficult, but it does take a good deal of extra concentration.

A greater hazard than starting on the right is complacency once you have become used to it and start to feel comfortable with it. It is all too easy to revert to ingrained habit, and pull out on to the wrong side, particularly after a stop, for fuel, for a meal, or overnight. Before driving off again, remind yourself to pull out on the correct side. Stick a note on the dashboard, or make it a family habit that every time you drive off again after stopping, everyone reminds you 'Drive on the right!'

Take care not to make the mistake one very experienced motoring writer friend of mine once did, with unfortunate consequences. At the end of a French holiday, he pulled out of a filling station on to the right-hand side of the road. But by this time he was back home in England, and collided with another car. A habit ingrained from a couple of weeks on the Continent had taken over.

What to take with you

You must carry your driving licence, and an international licence if you are driving through or to a country such as Spain where it is a requirement. But there are other documents you must also take when driving abroad:

➜ A copy of the vehicle registration document (a photocopy is acceptable).

➜ Written confirmation from the owner that you are driving the car abroad with their permission, if the car you are driving is borrowed, hired or leased.

➔ A green card to extend your insurance cover: your British motor insurance policy covers you in other EC countries, but normally only for third party risks, even if the cover is fully comprehensive at home. Give your insurance company plenty of notice (ideally at least a month), and be prepared for an extra charge.

➔ A bail bond, if your destination is Spain, available from your motor insurer or motoring organisation. Without one you risk landing in gaol if you are involved in an accident.

➔ A warning triangle, which is compulsory in many countries. A fire extinguisher and a first aid kit are also compulsory in a few countries, but it makes sense to have them anyway.

➔ Have a door mirror fitted on the nearside, if your car doesn't already have one. They are compulsory in Italy, but are helpful for driving on the right anyway.

➔ A GB plate – compulsory in many countries, where failing to display one could make you liable for an on-the-spot fine.

➔ Although not compulsory it is advisable to take out breakdown and medical insurance cover to deal with any emergencies which may arise abroad. If you or someone in the car were taken ill or involved in a crash, the cost of an air ambulance home could be prohibitively expensive without insurance. Also when about to travel in the EC, obtain E111 forms for each person in the car. You can get them in advance of your trip from Post Offices, and once they have been completed and authorised, they ensure that you are eligible for medical treatment abroad under EC rules.

➔ Don't only take currency of the country you are heading for, but also carry a reasonable amount of cash in the relevant local currency for any country through which you are driving, to deal with any problems that may arise.

➔ Carry an emergency spares kit in case parts are not readily available while you are away, especially a set of spare bulbs for all the car's lights.

Finally, think of your return. Even if you have booked your ferry or hovercraft crossing, it is worth taking a timetable, so that if your plans have to change for some reason, you can plan accordingly.

Preparing for your trip

DO ✔

✔ Ensure that your car's lights are converted so that the dipped beam does not dazzle oncoming drivers abroad. Most service stations sell masks to attach to the headlights, with directions for all common makes of car.

✔ Have the car serviced to reduce the risk of a breakdown while you are away.

✔ Learn the terms for different types of petrol in the countries you are visiting. Take special care over this if your car has a catalytic converter and must use only unleaded, or if it has a diesel engine.

DON'T ✗

✗ Overload the car, both for safety and comfort reasons, and because an overladen vehicle risks a fine and could invalidate your insurance.

✗ Cut timings too fine and find yourself in a rush to catch a ferry or reach an overnight stop at a reasonable hour. Being in a hurry in unfamiliar driving conditions is a recipe for trouble.

✗ Expect to be able to indulge too liberally in the heady freedom of higher speed limits. On-the-spot fines can be a big drain on the holiday budget.

The law

Drink-drive limits

Most European countries have a blood-alcohol limit similar to the one in Britain, namely 80 mg of alcohol per 100 ml of blood. But there are some exceptions where a lower limit applies:

50 mg/100 ml: France, Finland, Greece, Holland, Norway, Portugal, Yugoslavia.

20 mg/100 ml: Poland, Sweden.

20 mg/100 ml: Bulgaria, Czechoslovakia, eastern part of Germany (former GDR), Hungary, Romania, Turkey, USSR.

Driving age limits

Most countries impose a minimum age of 18 at which a British licence-holder may drive a temporarily imported car. The exceptions in which a visiting driver aged 17 may drive are Denmark, Germany, Greece, Luxembourg, Norway, and Portugal.

Speed limits

Across Europe the normal speed limits are 50 k/h (31 mph) in urban areas, 100 k/h (62 mph) elsewhere, and130 k/h (81 mph) on motorways.

There are exceptions, so beware of local limits and watch the signs. Some countries also have minimum speed limits on certain roads, so check with your travel agent or motor organisation before you go.

On-the-spot fines are common throughout much of Europe and can be heavy. Being caught for a speeding offence on the Continent can leave you £100 poorer, and the police imposing the fine may not necessarily accept credit card payment but may insist on cash.

Speed limits in mph
Speed limits are quoted in kilometres per hour. These are the approximate conversions:

30 k/h – 18 mph	70 k/h – 43 mph	110 k/h – 68 mph
40 k/h – 24 mph	80 k/h – 50 mph	120 k/h – 74 mph
50 k/h – 31 mph	90 k/h – 56 mph	130 k/h – 81 mph
60 k/h – 37 mph	100 k/h – 62 mph	

Seat belt regulations

In most European countries it is compulsory for drivers and passengers to wear seat belts. In many of them young children are not permitted to travel in the front passenger seat, and the law specifies that they must be strapped in. Check local regulations.

Points to note country by country

The following details are not exhaustive, but do give the main legal and practical differences in motoring law and practice in Europe.

Austria

➜ Children under twelve not allowed in front seat unless using a special child seat or harness.

➜ Warning triangle and first aid kit compulsory.

➜ Credit cards not usually accepted at filling stations.

➜ Speed limits 50 k/h urban, 100 k/h rural, 130 k/h motorways.

Belgium

➜ Children under twelve not allowed in front except in special child seat.

➜ Warning triangle compulsory.

➜ Speed limits 60 k/h urban, 90 k/h rural, 120 k/h motorways.

➜ Minimum speed of 70 k/h on motorways.

Denmark

➜ Dipped headlights compulsory in daylight driving.

➜ Children over three and under seven must be secured in child restraints; legal recommendation that children under three be strapped into baby seat.

➜ Warning triangle compulsory.

➜ Line of white triangles across road indicates you must stop and give way.

➜ Speed limits 50 k/h urban, 80 k/h rural, 100 k/h motorways.

Finland

➡ Dipped headlights compulsory in daylight driving outside built-up areas.

➡ Warning triangle not compulsory for visitors, but 'strongly advised'.

➡ Speed limits 50 k/h urban, 80–100 k/h rural (maximum 80 k/h where there are no signs), 120 k/h motorways. On roads surfaced with gravel or loose stones, reduce speed to between 30–50 k/h.

France (and Monaco)

➡ Seat belt wearing compulsory.

➡ Children under ten not permitted in the front seat.

➡ Speed limits 50 k/h urban, 90 k/h rural, 110 k/h dual carriageways, 130 k/h motorways. Minimum speed in outside lane on motorways in good weather is 80 k/h.

➡ Special speed limits apply in wet weather: 80 k/h rural, 100 k/h dual carriageways, 110 k/h motorways.

➡ Any driver who has held a full licence for less than a year must not exceed 90 kph at any time.

➡ Warning triangle or hazard warning lights compulsory. Recommended to carry a set of spare replacement light bulbs.

➡ On roundabouts with no signs specifying who has priority, it is with traffic entering the roundabout. Traffic already on the roundabout takes priority where there are signs to warn drivers approaching the roundabout that 'Vous n'avez pas la priorité' or' 'Cédez le passage'.

Germany

➡ Seat belt wearing compulsory.

➡ Children under twelve not permitted in the front unless using suitable child safety equipment.

➡ Illegal, and can earn an on-the-spot fine, to run out of petrol on a motorway, use abusive language or make derogatory signs while driving.

➡ Warning triangle mandatory, first-aid kit recommended.

➡ Slow moving vehicles must by law stop and let others past.

➡ Speed limits are 50 k/h urban, 100 k/h rural, recommended but not always mandatory 130 k/h on dual carriageways and motorways.

➡ Speed limits in the former East Germany or GDR until 31 December 1992 are 80 k/h rural, 100 k/h motorways.

Gibraltar

➔ Seat belt wearing not compulsory but 'strongly recommended'.

➔ Use of full-beam headlamps prohibited.

➔ Using car horn forbidden within city limits.

➔ Filling stations do not take credit cards.

➔ Speed limit 30 k/h inside city, 50 k/h outside.

Greece

➔ Seat belt wearing compulsory in front.

➔ Children under ten forbidden to travel in front seat.

➔ Fines for unnecessary use of car horn.

➔ Warning triangle, first aid kit and fire extinguisher compulsory.

➔ Carrying petrol in a can in the car is illegal.

➔ Few filling stations take credit cards.

➔ Speed limits 50 k/h urban, 80 k/h rural, 100 k/h motorways.

Holland

➔ Seat belt wearing compulsory in front seats.

➔ Children under12 not permitted in front except for a child under four in special baby seat, or a child over four using seat belt which does not cross the chest.

➔ Compulsory to carry warning triangle outside built-up areas.

➔ Buses have right of way leaving bus-stops in urban areas.

➔ Speed limits 50 k/h urban, 80 k/h rural, 120 k/h motorways. Minimum speed on motorways 70 k/h.

➔ Be prepared for a large numbers of cyclists.

Italy

➔ You must carry an official translation of your driving licence if you have a traditional green British one. Translations are available at border posts or in advance from the AA or RAC. It is not necessary with a pink EC style British licence.

➔ Dipped headlights mandatory when driving through road tunnels even where they are well lit.

➔ Seat belt wearing compulsory.

➔ Children under ten not permitted in the front seat unless wearing child safety restraint.

➔ Children under four can only travel in the back if wearing safety restraint.

➔ Warning triangle compulsory.

➜ Carrying spare can of petrol in the car is illegal.

➜ Petrol is dear in Italy and motorway tolls can be costly. A concessionary package of petrol coupons, motorway toll card and breakdown assistance can be bought from border offices.

➜ Speed limits 50 k/h urban, 90 k/h rural. On motorways the limit is 110 k/h for cars below 1100 cc, 130 k/h for cars 1100 cc and above.

Luxembourg

➜ After dark parked cars must have sidelights on where there is no public lighting.

➜ When overtaking outside built-up areas at night, it is compulsory to flash your headlights as a warning.

➜ Seat belt wearing compulsory.

➜ Children under ten are only allowed in front if strapped into a child safety seat, and are not permitted to ride in front when a seat is available in the back.

➜ Use of warning triangle in a breakdown is compulsory.

➜ It is illegal to carry petrol in a spare can.

➜ Speed limits are 60 k/h urban, 90 k/h rural, 120 k/h motorways.

Norway

➜ Dipped headlamps compulsory for daytime driving.

➜ Seat belt wearing compulsory, no age limit on front seat passenger as long as the belt fits.

➜ City tolls must be paid when driving into Oslo or Bergen.

➜ Speed limits are 50 k/h urban, 80-90 k/h rural roads and motorways (as indicated on signs).

Portugal

➜ Seat belt wearing compulsory in the front when driving outside built-up areas.

➜ Children under 12 not permitted in front unless using special child restraints.

➜ Warning triangle compulsory.

➜ Speed limits are 60 k/h urban, 90 k/h rural, 120 k/h motorways.

➜ If you have had a driving licence for less than a year you must not exceed 90 k/h on any road, and must display on the back of the car a yellow '90' disc (car accessory shops in Portugal sell them).

Spain

→ Seat belt wearing is compulsory outside built-up areas, and on ring roads around large towns or cities.

→ Children under 12 not permitted in the front seat unless using suitable child safety restraints.

→ International driving permit bearing your photograph is compulsory. It can be obtained in advance from the AA or RAC.

→ Spare set of replacement bulbs for car lights must be carried.

→ Few filling stations take credit cards.

→ Speed limits 60 k/h urban, 90–100 k/h rural, 120 k/h motorways.

Sweden

→ Dipped headlights mandatory for driving in daylight.

→ Seat belt wearing compulsory.

→ Children under seven must use child safety seat or suitable safety restraints.

→ Wild moose and reindeer a serious road safety hazard: about one in five road accidents in Sweden involves collision with one.

→ Speed limits are 50 k/h urban, 70 k/h rural, 90–110 k/h dual carriageways and motorways.

Switzerland

→ Seat belt wearing compulsory in front.

→ Children under 12 only permitted in front if wearing suitable child safety restraint, and must ride in back if space available.

→ Dipped headlights are compulsory in road tunnels even where well-lit.

→ Warning triangle compulsory.

→ Fixed toll charge to use motorways must be paid (30 Swiss francs, valid for 1 year) and sticker displayed on the car. Can be bought in advance from the AA or RAC, or at the border.

→ Speed limits 50 k/h urban, 80 k/h rural, 120 k/h motorways.

Yugoslavia

→ Seat belt wearing compulsory.

→ Children under 12 not allowed in front seat.

→ Warning triangle (two if towing trailer), first aid kit and replacement bulbs kit compulsory.

→ Any visible damage to the car when entering the country must be certified by border authorities and a certificate obtained, which must be produced when leaving.

➜ Fuel and motorway toll coupons can be bought at the frontier.

➜ Speed limits 60 k/h urban, 80 k/h rural, 100 k/h dual carriageways, 120 k/h motorways.

Crossing the channel

Planning a holiday trip in not necessarily a simple matter of choosing the nearest port and heading for it. Crossing times vary from between about half an hour, on the hovercraft from Dover, to around 9.5 hours on the overnight Plymouth/Roscoff ferry.

Deciding which route to choose will depend on where you are heading for on the other side, as well as how close you live to one of the ports on this side.

The chart below gives approximate crossing times, plus the distances by road from French ports to a variety of popular destinations.

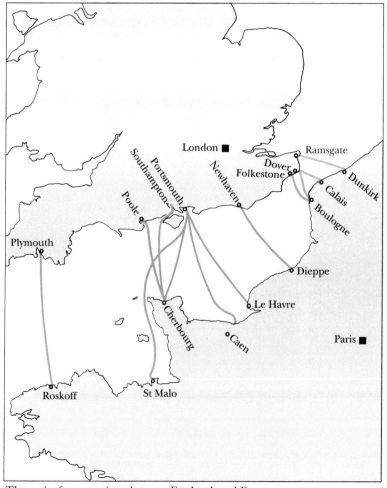

The main ferry crossings between England and France.

	Approximate Crossing Time	Miles from continental port									
		Paris	St Tropez	Biarritz	Avignon	Nancy	Perpignan	Geneva	Vienna	Rome	Barcelona
Ramsgate/Dunkirk	2hrs 30 mins	192	751	683	623	316	760	529	803	1037	874
Dover/Calais	1hr 30 mins	184	743	675	615	302	752	721	820	1045	866
Dover/Boulogne	1hr 20 mins	189	748	680	620	308	757	626	834	1050	871
Folkstone/Boulogne	1hr 50 mins	189	748	680	620	308	757	526	834	1050	871
Newhaven/Dieppe	4hrs	102	679	549	551	306	688	457	856	1003	802
Portsmouth/Le Havre	5hrs 45 mins (day) 7hrs 45 mins – 8hrs (night)	127	681	551	553	323	690	459	896	1006	804
Portsmouth/Caen	5hrs 45 mins	158	712	496	584	354	656	490	927	1037	770
Portsmouth/Cherbourg	4hrs 45 mins (day) 8hrs 30 mins – 8hrs 45 mins (night)	224	778	511	650	420	670	556	993	1102	784
Portsmouth/St Malo	9 hrs	247	780	447	652	432	606	558	1012	1104	720
Southampton/Cherbourg	6hrs (day) 8hrs (night)	224	778	511	650	420	670	556	993	1102	784
Poole/Cherbourg	4hrs 30 mins	224	778	511	650	420	670	556	993	1102	784
Plymouth/Roscoff	5hrs 4 mins – 6hrs 30 minutes day) 8rs 15 mins – 9hrs 30 mins (night)	350	882	538	754	535	698	660	1114	1207	812

Fault finding

Help. The car won't start. The temperature shoots up. The engine suddenly loses power. What do I do next?

Many drivers, confronted by a problem with the car and unsure how to tackle it, will simply summon a breakdown service or call in a local garage to sort out the problem. But it can be very satisfying to first try and analyse for yourself what may be wrong, either to make some effort to sort it out, or to have some idea of what you may be dealing with before calling for assistance.

The engine will not start

1. Is there not even a sound of the starter motor turning? Then it may be defective, or the battery is completely flat. Switch on the headlamps. If they are 'dead', you have a flat battery.

2. Does the starter motor whirr very sluggishly and the lights go dim? Sounds like a nearly-flat battery, in need of recharging.

3. Is there a clicking sound from under the bonnet? You could have a loose battery connection. Check the terminals are clean and tight, and try again.

4. Do the headlights stay bright as you try the starter? If they do there could be a loose electrical connection somewhere.

5. Does the starter motor turn normally, the lights stay bright, but the engine show no sign of wanting to fire? You may have damp in the electrics, in which case it could be curable with a damp-repellant aerosol spray.

6. After trying the starter for some time, can you smell petrol? The engine may be 'flooded'. Wait a few minutes, then slowly press the accelerator pedal right down, keep the choke right in, and try again.

7. After performing normally on a long drive in hot weather, does the car fail to start after a brief stop? It may be due to petrol vaporisation in the fuel line. Wait at least 20 minutes with the bonnet open and then try again.

The car starts to smell hot

Never ignore symptoms of overheating, which are potentially hazardous for the car and possibly for you, too.

1. Does the interior start to feel steamy and the temperature gauge rise? The engine is starting to boil, most likely due to a fault in the cooling system. Stop and let it cool down, and after at least 15 minutes top it up.

2. Does the car overheat again after you have refilled the cooling system and driven cautiously on? Check for a loose fan-belt or any split hoses. If those seem fine, it could be a faulty thermostat or water pump. Do not try and drive any further; summon help.

3. Do you detect a singeing smell and notice the car feeling hot? Stop, but do not fling open the bonnet to check for trouble. If something has started to smoulder, it could burst into flames. Cautiously open the bonnet a crack to see where the trouble is, and call for help.

The engine becomes noisy or loses power

1. Does the engine start to make a screeching sound? It could be trouble with the fan belt, water pump or dynamo bearings.

2. Do you suddenly notice a knocking sound under power? It might be trouble inside the engine. Stop and seek help.

3. Does the engine start cutting out? It may be a fault in the ignition system.

4. Does the engine splutter and misfire? If there is plenty of fuel in the tank, it could be a fault in the fuel feed to the engine.

5. Does the engine misfire and the temperature suddenly rise? Could be a blown head gasket. Stop immediately.

6. Does the engine sound normal and rev normally, but the power simply ebb away? It may well be a transmission problem.

Useful addresses

Motor manufacturers

ALFA ROMEO
Poulton Close
Dover
Kent CT17 OHP
Tel. 0753 690690

ASTON MARTIN
Tickford Street
Newport Pagnell
Buckinghamshire MK16 9AN
Tel. 0908 610620

AUDI
Yeomans Drive
Blakelands
Milton Keynes MK14 5HR
Tel. 0908 601187

BMW
Ellesfield Avenue
Bracknell
Berkshire RG12 4TA
Tel. 0344 426565

BRISTOL
368-370 Kensington High Street
London W14 8NL
Tel. 071-603 5556

CATERHAM
Seven House
Town End
Caterham Hill
Surrey CR3 5UG
Tel. 08833 46666

CITROËN
221 Bath Road
Slough
Berkshire SL1 4BA
Tel. 0753 822100

DACIA
Units 1-3 Artillery Road
Bofors Park
Yeovil
Somerset BA22 8RP
Tel. 0935 75666

DAIHATSU
Poulton Close
Dover
Kent CT17 OHP
Tel. 0304 213030

FERRARI
Crabtree Road
Thorpe Industrial Estate
Egham
Surrey TW20 8RJ
Tel. 0784 436222

FIAT
266 Bath Road
Slough
Berkshire SL1 4HJ
Tel. 0753 511431

FORD
Eagle Way Warley
Brentwood
Essex CM13 3BW
Tel. 0277 253000

FSO
77 Mount Ephraim
Tunbridge Wells
Kent TN4 8BS
Tel. 0892 511811

HONDA
4 Power Road
Chiswick
London W4 5YT
Tel. 081-747 1400

HYUNDAI
Ryder Street
West Bromwich
West Midlands B70 OEJ
Tel. 021-522 2000

JAGUAR
Browns Lane
Allesley
Coventry CV5 9DR
Tel. 0203 402121

LADA
Western House
Middle Lane
Wythall
Birmingham B47 6LA
Tel. 0564 824171

LANCIA
266 Bath Road
Slough
Berkshire SL1 4HJ
Tel. 0753 690690

LAND ROVER
Lode Lane
Solihull B92 8NW
Tel. 021-722 2424

LOTUS
Hethel
Norwich
Norfolk NR14 8EZ
Tel. 0953 608000

MAZDA
Mount Ephraim
Tunbridge Wells
Kent TN4 8BS
Tel. 0892 511877

MERCEDES-BENZ
Tongwell
Milton Keynes
Buckinghamshire MK15 8BA
Tel. 0908 678262

MITSUBISHI
Watermoor
Cirencester
Gloucestershire GL7 1LF
Tel. 0285 655777

MORGAN
Pickersleigh Road
Malvern Link
Worcestershire WR14 2LL
Tel. 0684 573104

NISSAN
Columbia Drive
Worthing
Sussex BN13 3HD
Tel. 0903 68561

PEUGEOT TALBOT
Aldermoor House
Aldermoor Lane
Coventry CV3 1LT
Tel. 0203 884000

PORSCHE
Bath Road
Calcot
Reading
Berkshire RG3 7SE
Tel. 0734 303666

PROTON
Western House
Middle Lane
Wythall
Birmingham B47 6LA
Tel. 0564 826167

RENAULT
Western Avenue
London W3 ORZ
Tel. 081-992 3481

ROLLS-ROYCE & BENTLEY
Pyms Lane
Crewe
Cheshire CW1 3PL
Tel. 0270 255155

ROVER
Canley Road
Coventry CV5 6QX
Tel. 0203 670111

SAAB
Saab House
Globe Park
Marlow
Buckinghamshire SL7 1LY
Tel. 0628 486977

SEAT
Gatwick Road
Crawley
West Sussex RH10 2AX
Tel. 0293 514141

SKODA
150 Goswell Road
London EC1V 7DS
Tel. 071-253 7441

SUZUKI
46-62 Gatwick Road
Crawley
West Sussex RH10 2XF
Tel. 0293 518000

TOYOTA
The Quadrangle
Redhill
Surrey RH1 1PX
Tel. 0737 768585

TVR
Bristol Avennue
Blackpool
Lancashire FY2 OJF
Tel. 0253 56151

VAUXHALL
Griffin House
Osborne Road
Luton LU1 3YT
Tel. 0582 21122

VOLKSWAGEN
Yeomans Drive
Blakelands
Milton Keynes MK14 5HR
Tel. 0908 601187

VOLVO
Globe Park
Marlow
Buckinghamshire SL7 1YQ
Tel. 06284 77977

Motoring organisations

AA
Fanum House
Basingstoke
Hampshire RG21 2EA
Tel. 0256 20123

ENVIRONMENTAL
TRANSPORT ASSOCIATION
17 George Street
Croydon
Surrey CRO 1LA
Tel. 081-666 0445

EUROP ASSISTANCE
252 High Street
Croydon
Surrey CRO 1NF
Tel. 081-680 1234

GUILD OF EXPERIENCED
MOTORISTS
Station Road
Forest Row
East Sussex RH18 5EN
Tel. 0342 825676

INSTITUTE OF ADVANCED
MOTORISTS
IAM House
359-365 Chiswick High Road
London W4 4HS
Tel. 081-994 4403

MONDIAL ASSISTANCE
201-204 High Street
Croydon
Surrey CRO 1AX
Tel. 081-681 2525

NATIONAL BREAKDOWN
RECOVERY CLUB
PO Box 300
Leeds LS99 2LZ
Tel. 0532 393545

RAC
M1 Cross
Brent Terrace
London NW2 1LT
Tel. 081-452 8000

ROYAL SCOTTISH
AUTOMOBILE CLUB
11 Blythswood Square
Glasgow G2 4AG
Tel. 041-221 3850

ROYAL SOCIETY FOR THE
PREVENTION OF
ACCIDENTS
Cannon House
Priory Queensway
Birmingham
Tel. 021-233 2461

*Industry, trade
organisations*
RETAIL MOTOR INDUSTRY
FEDERATION
201 Great Portland Street
London W1N 6AB
Tel. 071-580 9122

SCOTTISH MOTOR TRADE
ASSOCIATION
3 Palmerston Place
Edinburgh EH12 5AF
Tel. 031-225 3643

SOCIETY OF MOTOR
MANUFACTURERS AND
TRADERS
Forbes House
Halkin Street
London SW1X 7DS
Tel. 071-235 7000

Consumer organisations
CONSUMERS ASSOCIATION
2 Marylebone Road
London NW1 4DX
Tel. 071-486 5544

NATIONAL CONSUMER
COUNCIL
20 Grosvenor House
London SW1W ODYH
Tel. 071-0730 3469

Legislation, licences
DEPARTMENT OF
TRANSPORT
2 Marsham Street
London SW1P 3EB
Tel. 071-276 3000

DRIVER AND VEHICLE
LICENSING AGENCY
Longview Road
Morriston
Swansea SA6 7JL
Tel. 0792 782363

Oil companies

BP
Breakspear Way
Hemel Hempstead
Hertfordshire HP2 4UL
Tel. 0442 225226

CASTROL
Pipers Way
Swindon
Wiltshire SN3 1RE
Tel. 0793 512712

DUCKHAMS
157-159 Masons Hill
Bromley
Kent BR2 9HU
Tel. 081-290 0600

ESSO
Victoria Street
London SW1E 5JW
Tel. 071-834 6677

GULF
The Quadrangle
Imperial Square
Cheltenham
Gloucestershire GL50 1TF
Tel. 0242 225225

SHELL
Shell-Mex House Strand
London WC2R ODX
Tel. 071-257 3333

TEXACO
1 Knightsbridge Green
London SW1X 7QJ
Tel. 071-584 5000

TOTAL
4 Lancer Square
London W8 4EW
Tel. 071-937 7777

Tyre companies

AVON
Bath Road
Melksham
Wiltshire SN12 8AA
Tel. 0225 703101

BRIDGESTONE
Birchley Trading Estate
Oldbury
Warley
West Midlands B69 1DT
Tel. 021-552 3331

CONTINENTAL
4-8 High Street
West Drayton
Middlesex UB7 7DJ
Tel. 0895 445678

FIRESTONE
Fairfield Avenue
Staines
Middlesex TW18 4BA
Tel. 0784 465651

GOODYEAR
Stafford Road
Wolverhampton
West Midlands WV10 6DH
Tel. 0902 22321

MICHELIN
Davy House
Lyon Road
Harrow
Middlesex HA1 2DQ
Tel. 081-861 2121

PIRELLI
Derby Road
Burton-on-Trent
Staffordshire DE13 OBH
Tel. 0283 66301

SP TYRES
Fort Dunlop
Birmingham B24 9QT
Tel. 021-384 4444

UNIROYAL
4-8 High Street
West Drayton
Middlesex UB7 7DJ
Tel. 0895 445678

Insurance Association
Association of British Insurers
Aldermary House
10-15 Queen Street
London EC4N 1TT
Tel. 071-248 4477

Caravanning
CAMPING AND
CARAVANNING CLUB
Greenfields House
Westwood Way,
Coventry CV4 8JH
Tel. 0203 694995

CARAVAN CLUB
East Grinstead House
East Grinstead
West Sussex RH19 1UA
Tel.0342 326944

Disabled drivers
DISABLED MOTORISTS
FEDERATION
National Mobility Centre
Unit 2A Atcham Estate
Shrewsbury
Shropshire SY4 4UG
Tel. 0743 761889

Motor Shows
EARLS COURT
Exhibition Centre
Warwick Road
London SW5 9TA
Tel. 071-385 1200
(Motorfair, autumn 1993 and
following alternate years)

NATIONAL EXHIBITION
CENTRE
Birmingham B40 1NT
Tel. 021-780 4141
(Motor Show, autumn 1992 and
following alternate years)

Museum
NATIONAL MOTOR
MUSEUM
Beaulieu
Hampshire SO42 7ZN
Tel. 0590 612345

Motor racing circuits
BRANDS HATCH
Fawkham
Near Dartford
Kent DA3 8NG
Tel. 0474 872331

DONINGTON PARK
Castle Donington
Derby DE7 2RP
Tel. 0332 810048

SILVERSTONE
Near Towcester
Northamptonshire NN12 8TN
Tel. 0327 857271

THRUXTON
Andover
Hampshire SP11 8PN
Tel. 0264 772607

Ferry, hovercraft companies

BRITANNY FERRIES
The Britanny Centre
Whard Road
Portsmouth PO2 8RU
Tel. 0705 827701

HOVERSPEED
International Hoverport
Western Docks
Dover
Kent CT17 9TG
Tel. 0304 240101

P&O EUROPEAN FERRIES
Channel House
Channel View Road Dover
Kent CT17 9TJ
Tel. 0304 223833

SEALINK STELLA LINE
Sea Containers House
20 Upper Ground
London SE1 9PF
Tel. 071-928 5550

Accessories, car care and repair products

HALFORDS
Icknield Street Drive
Washford West
Redditch
Worcestershire B98 0DE
Tel. 0527 517601

HALFORDS HELPLINE
SERVICE
For locations of nearest stores
Tel. 081-200 0200

Answers to the road signs on page 67
From left to right, top to bottom Level crossing *without gate or barrier,* no vehicles, two-way traffic crosses one-way road, no motor vehicles, steep uphill gradient, clearway (no stopping).

Index

£1 OFF

any Haynes Manual

To the Customer:
This voucher is only valid when purchasing a Haynes manual. Only one voucher may be redeemed per item purchased. This voucher cannot be exchanged for cash or any other item. Not to be used in conjunction with any other offer. Offer closes 13.5.92.

Voucher Code No:
022840

To the Branch:
Treat as a cash voucher as per Till Operators' Guide p.9 and Managers' Till Guide p.5.

£10 OFF

any Radio Cassette Unit (over £100)

To the Customer:
This voucher is only valid when purchasing a Radio Cassette Unit over £100. Only one voucher may be redeemed per item purchased. This voucher cannot be exchanged for cash or any other item. Not to be used in conjunction with any other offer. Offer closes 13.5.92.

Voucher Code No:
022933

To the Branch:
Treat as a cash voucher as per Till Operators' Guide p.9 and Managers' Till Guide p.5.

£1 OFF
any Haynes Manual

To the Customer:
This voucher is only valid when purchasing a Haynes manual. Only one voucher may be redeemed per item purchased. This voucher cannot be exchanged for cash or any other item. Not to be used in conjunction with any other offer. Offer closes 13.5.92.

Voucher Code No:
022840

To the Branch:
Treat as a cash voucher as per Till Operators' Guide p.9 and Managers' Till Guide p.5.

£10 OFF
any Radio Cassette Unit (over £100)

To the Customer:
This voucher is only valid when purchasing a Radio Cassette Unit over £100. Only one voucher may be redeemed per item purchased. This voucher cannot be exchanged for cash or any other item. Not to be used in conjunction with any other offer. Offer closes 13.5.92.

Voucher Code No:
022933

To the Branch:
Treat as a cash voucher as per Till Operators' Guide p.9 and Managers' Till Guide p.5.

£5 OFF

Halford's 75 piece Tool Set

To the Customer:
This voucher is only valid when purchasing a Halford's 75 piece Tool Set. Only one voucher may be redeemed per item purchased. This voucher cannot be exchanged for cash or any other item. Not to be used in conjunction with any other offer.
Offer closes 13.5.92.

Voucher Code No:
023025
Item Code 416321

To the Branch:
Treat as a cash voucher as per Till Operators' Guide p.9 and Managers' Till Guide p.5.

£10 OFF

Halford's Roof Box

To the Customer:
This voucher is only valid when purchasing a Halford's Roof Box. Only one voucher may be redeemed per item purchased. This voucher cannot be exchanged for cash or any other item. Not to be used in conjunction with any other offer.
Offer closes 13.5.92.

THANK HALFORDS FOR THAT

Voucher Code No:
023126
Item Code 474536

To the Branch:
Treat as a cash voucher as per Till Operators' Guide p.9 and Managers' Till Guide p.5.

£20 OFF

KARCHER K580 PRESSURE WASHER

To the Customer:
This voucher is only valid when purchasing a Karcher Pressure Washer. Only one voucher may be redeemed per item purchased. This voucher cannot be exchanged for cash or any other item. Not to be used in conjunction with any other offer.
Offer closes 13.5.92.

Voucher Code No:
022624
Item Code 600643

To the Branch:
Treat as a cash voucher as per Till Operators' Guide p.9 and Managers' Till Guide p.5.

£5 OFF

Halford's 75 piece Tool Set

To the Customer:
This voucher is only valid when purchasing a Halford's 75 piece Tool Set. Only one voucher may be redeemed per item purchased. This voucher cannot be exchanged for cash or any other item. Not to be used in conjunction with any other offer.
Offer closes 13.5.92.

Voucher Code No:
023025
Item Code 416321

To the Branch:
Treat as a cash voucher as per Till Operators' Guide p.9 and Managers' Till Guide p.5.

£10 OFF

Halford's Roof Box

To the Customer:
This voucher is only valid when purchasing a Halford's Roof Box. Only one voucher may be redeemed per item purchased. This voucher cannot be exchanged for cash or any other item. Not to be used in conjunction with any other offer.
Offer closes 13.5.92.

Voucher Code No:
023126
Item Code 474536

To the Branch:
Treat as a cash voucher as per Till Operators' Guide p.9 and Managers' Till Guide p.5.

£20 OFF

KARCHER K580 PRESSURE WASHER

To the Customer:
This voucher is only valid when purchasing a Karcher Pressure Washer. Only one voucher may be redeemed per item purchased. This voucher cannot be exchanged for cash or any other item. Not to be used in conjunction with any other offer.
Offer closes 13.5.92.

Voucher Code No:
022624
Item Code 600643

To the Branch:
Treat as a cash voucher as per Till Operators' Guide p.9 and Managers' Till Guide p.5.